THE SUPERNATURAL

Medieval Theological Concepts to Modern

THE SUPER natural

J.P. Kenny, S.J.

alba house

A DIVISION OF THE SOCIETY OF ST. PAUL
STATEN ISLAND, NEW YORK 10314

Library of Congress Cataloging in Publication Data

Kenny, John Peter, 1916-
    The supernatural.

    Bibliography: p.
    1. Supernatural—History of doctrines. I. Title.
BT745.K45   231   72-3575
ISBN   0-8189-0251-5

Nihil Obstat:
    William H. Winters, O.F.M. Cap., S.T.L.
    Censor Librorum

Imprimatur:
    James P. Mahoney
    Vicar General, Archdiocese of New York
    March 30, 1972

The nihil obstat and imprimatur are official declarations that
a book or pamphlet is free of doctrinal or moral error. No
implication is contained therein that those who have granted
the nihil obstat and imprimatur agree with the contents, opinions
or statements expressed.

Designed, printed and bound in the U.S.A. by the
Pauline Fathers and Brothers of the Society
of St. Paul, 2187 Victory Blvd., Staten Island, N.Y.
10314 as part of their communications apostolate.

MATRI   BENEVOLENTI
BEATAE   MARIAE   VIRGINI
FILIALI   PIETATE
FIDELITER
DEDICATUM

CONTENTS

Introduction

IN Roman Catholic theology, the term: *supernatural* is the
acknowledged and legitimate child of scholasticism. Hence
it shares in the current strong disfavor with which scholasticism is treated on all hands, as much inside as outside Roman
Catholicism. Especially younger thinkers resolutely reject its
static, depersonalized presentation of the Good News. They
likewise extend their disapproval to the technical term that
scholasticism uses to cover the sublime reality of man's divinization and of his insertion in the mystery of Christ. At present
supernatural still enjoys the prestige of being an indispensable
code-word of Roman Catholic theology. However, it is unlikely
that it will long survive the eclipse of the system that begot it.
Some other term (perhaps *Mystery of Christ?*) will perhaps
supplant it. But whatever verdict is finally pronounced on
scholasticism together with its armory of technical expressions,
we shall always need to enrich ourselves by studying the
history of theological ideas. We shall understand much better
what modern theology is trying to do and assess with nicer
discrimination and sobriety its eventual achievement, if we
have assisted at the birth and growth of the theology of the
supernatural during the millennium of scholasticism. It is to be
hoped that this slim volume can render some service here.

Our aim is deliberately narrowed to two points: (i)—
briefly and, at the same time, as comprehensively as possible
to survey the unfolding scholastic theology of the supernatural; (ii)—to note and comment on the reaction it has
provoked among twentieth century thinkers.

Consonant with our precise aim, we offer the reader no investigation of the biblical sources of this dogma, nor do we attempt to trace its ramifications throughout the patristic period. We are aware that, in the course of 2000 years, the magisterium of the Church has intervened at least nine times in a fashion significant for the theology of the supernatural. We have refused to be sidetracked into a discussion of these interventions—merely referring to one or other of them as the occasion seemed to demand.

This volume comprises seven chapters. The first deals with the definition of the technical concept of the supernatural according to the scholastic perspective. Chapters 2, 3, 4 and 5 follow the development of the theology of the supernatural throughout the four great phases of scholasticism: early, high, late and post-tridentine.° The sixth chapter returns once more to the technical term, tracing its lineage, the circumstances favoring its growth and the nuancing of its meaning. The last chapter deals with the twentieth century reaction, above all in its most colorful and prophetic figure: Teilhard de Chardin.

° Cultures and currents of thought cannot be precisely dated. Still less can one be exact about phases within the particular culture. Thus St. Albert the Great (ob. 1280) and Alexander of Hales (ob. 1245) joined the dawning with the heyday of scholasticism. Likewise in Duns Scotus (ob. 1308) high and late scholasticism overlapped. Our aim in these four chapters will simply be to give a rough sketch of the salient characteristics of the theology of the supernatural in each phase of scholasticism.

THE SUPERNATURAL

Chapter 1

Definition

In this opening chapter we thrust a definition of the supernatural under the eyes of our reader. Today such aprioristic behavior is hardly fashionable, seems unmannerly and therefore calls for an explanation. The reader of a theological monograph on *man, God, Spirit, grace, Church,* or many other themes might feel justifiably incensed if the author, instead of interrogating the sources of revelation, began with a pre-fabricated definition. However, in the case of supernatural one cannot begin with the sources, because the term is sought in vain in both OT and NT. It is moreover lacking to the patristic literature of the first centuries and to the ancient liturgical texts. To achieve status as a technical term it needed not only centuries of theological reflection and maturation but also the importation into, and integration with Christian thought of the complex Aristotelic system of philosophy. After its shaping in the thirteenth century as a technical term, supernatural gradually grew in currency until, with the last three centuries, it became installed at the center of dogmatic theology.

But though the technical term itself is a relatively late

comer on the theological scene, the realities covered by it
figure everywhere in tradition and Scripture and belong to
the heart of Christianity. In fact supernatural vies with *incarnation, sacrament* or *revelation* in importance.

In popular language and literature, supernatural has a
wide application. It covers whatever is beyond the ken
of the senses or cannot be accounted for at the bar of physical science and empirical observation; whatever is metaphysical or transcendent or baffling to the rationalist or outside the routine workings of cause and effect. Supernatural
is a label popularly put on ghosts, angels or devils, God,
miracles and prodigies, things monstrous, portentous and
violent. In short all superior substances and surpassing effects
are commonly dubbed supernatural.

Our concern, of course, is not with the supernatural in
this ordinary, broad, indiscriminate meaning; rather we seek
to determine its technical theological sense. Straightway
one is confronted with a fluidity of terminology and with a
web of fine-spun distinctions so characteristic of scholastic
manuals. Scholastics like to link supernatural with one or
other of the following qualifications:—simply, absolutely, substantially, ontologically, entitatively, under certain respects,
relatively, to a certain degree. It is not our intention to dally
over these. Instead let us briefly contrast supernatural against
natural and preternatural and so make ready for the enuncia-
tion of our definition.

Natural describes the inborn resources and capacity of a
thing, or whatever is within the range and scope of its nature,
or whatever belongs to its own orbit. Thus it is natural for a
tree to grow but it is not natural for it to sing like a canary
or graze like a cow. It is natural for a bird to fly or chirp;
it is not natural for it to joke and laugh.

Preternatural presents the mezzanine stage between the
natural below and the supernatural above it. Or it regards

gifts that rise above and beyond purely native endowments but at the same time fall far below the characteristically divine sphere of the supernatural. Preternatural gifts are signalled by a double gratuity: they share the gratuity common to everything created and contingent; they join to this the special gratuity of outstripping the claims and demands of the particular nature they embellish. Examples: miraculous powers of healing; superhuman gifts of clairvoyance, prophecy, infallibility of tongues; the immunity from death and concupiscence which scholastic (though not many modern) theologians commonly attribute to "Adam" before his fall. Such gifts, while unowed, exceptional and undoubtedly indicative of a certain divine predilection, do not of themselves imply the descent of the divine into the human heart and are not unfailing signs of high personal holiness. Their tendency is to heighten and enhance the natural within its own domain and according to its own inmost drive and capabilities. Thus bodily immortality answers man's deep-seated, imperious longing for everlastingness; the perfect poise and self-mastery of integrity represents the target towards which all Christian asceticism is struggling; a disease miraculously cured is a natural restorative function omnipotently buttressed and accelerated.

Supernatural is quite other than natural and preternatural. It is not merely what is not natural and preternatural; it is much more than that; it is positively and wholly different. Supernatural can never be the natural endowment or prerequisite or prize of any creature whatsoever, real or imaginary. It is utterly inaccessible to the entire province of what is created or "creatable." It is uniquely and sovereignly gratuitous and essentially transcendent. Its hall-mark is the intrinsically divine. This characteristic, however, does not warrant our imagining that the supernatural is *Deus absconditus*, God in his own infinity, barricaded (as it were) behind

his own olympian remoteness and absoluteness. The supernatural is a relative rather than an absolute. It leans out
towards man and is for him. It implies a new relationship, a
fresh contact between God and man, a divine descent in
view of personal communion with man. Hence in its technical sense, supernatural always involves the pre-existence of
its term and indeed of the Universe. This does not necessarily
mean that a time-lag must divide man's creation from his
elevation. Both may happen together. Nevertheless creation
enjoys a priority of order and logic, which must be respected—
otherwise man's elevation is rendered unintelligible. This priority is allegorically and felicitously hinted at in Gn 2 where
Yahweh is pictured as first molding man in a desert and
then transporting him to Eden, symbol of a state of privilege.
Both the patristic and the Thomist traditions maintain that
Adam had original justice bestowed on him from the moment
of his creation.

Here then is our definition of the supernatural in the technical theological sense. We formulate it in alternative ways
so as to accentuate various facets of what is substantially
one and the same:

> *Supernatural*: Man's incorporation into the mystery of
> Christ here in view of the beatific vision hereafter. *Or*:
> the self-communication of the three-personed God, out
> of personal love, to sinful man, in Christ and the Church,
> in view of heaven.

The supernatural is God giving God to man—which, plainly,
only God can do.

Comments

1) The supernatural goes beyond the level of making and

creating to that of interpersonal communion, dialogue, loving exchange. In the order of creation God gives me myself; in the supernatural, the Father gives me himself through his Son. In the order of creation, God is Creator, *Factor;* I am *creatus, ex nihilo factus.* In the supernatural, the Father is *Genitor,* his Son *genitus, non factus,* and I am re-born, re-newed (*renatus, regeneratus*) in that Son. In the order of creation God produces things by way of efficient causality. In the supernatural God establishes a union with man in the field of "quasi-formal" causality. In the order of creation there is the bond of lord and servant, owner and chattel, artist and the child of his mind. In the supernatural there is a union of friendship, familiarity and mutual, personal love—arising however not merely from mental attitudes, sympathy and affections but much rather from a sending of the Spirit, Who inwardly changes and ontologically renews and energizes man.[1]

2) In both forms of our definition we relate the supernatural to *adult man*—not because we wish to be exclusive, but rather because he is naturally our immediate concern. In fact God can give himself to all personal beings—therefore to babies who assuredly deserve to be classified as persons though as yet incapable of personal commitment; likewise to angels—if one acknowledges their existence. On this score post-Vatican II theologians do not always share the unruffled and unsophisti-cated certitude enjoyed by their scholastic colleagues of past centuries. The infra-personal world of stocks, stones, plants and animals is inevitably closed against the supernatural,

1. In the scholastic view of things, creation is pitted against re-demption and the supernatural. In the modern approach, creation is simply the first and remote manifestation of the love of the Father of mercies for men.

precisely because this involves at least the possibility of personal dialogue.

3) At its best (for it has degrees) the supernatural means a conscious incorporation into the mystery of Christ as this is presented by St. Paul, Ep 1:3-14. It is, then, the mystery of our redemption and of our adoption through Christ; of the indwelling Spirit and of our sanctification; of baptismal renewal and membership of the Church. It is justification already given (*nun,* Rm 5:9, 11; 3:26); it is everlasting life already possessed (Jn 3:15-21, 36) though of course awaiting the ultimate fulfillment of heaven (Rm 8:23-25; 1 Jn 3:2).

4) Conformably to the whole plan of the Incarnation, the supernatural regularly reaches man not only through sense-perceptible rites but also through insertion into a group—the holy People of God. Thus it is vested with a communitarian or ecclesial aspect. This is emphasized by Vatican II:

> God did not create man for life in isolation, but for the formation of social unity. So also "it has pleased God to make men holy and save them not merely as individuals, without any mutual bonds, but by making them into a single people, a people which acknowledges Him in truth and serves Him in holiness." So from the beginning of salvation history He has chosen men not just as individuals but as members of a certain community. Revealing His mind to them, God called these chosen ones "His people" (Ex 3:7-12), and, furthermore, made a covenant with them on Sinai.
>
> This communitarian character is developed and consummated in the work of Jesus Christ. For the very Word made flesh willed to share in the human fellowship.[2]

2. *Gaudium et Spes,* 32, Abbot, p. 230; cf. *Ad Gentes* 2 & 3, pp. 585-587.

5) *Self-communication*: The supernatural is nothing less than God's self-donation to a creature. Hence the initiative is exclusively his, for only God can give God. Hence too the description of the supernatural as intrinsically divine in character. Primarily the supernatural is not some*thing* but some*body*. It is first and foremost an Uncreated Gift—the Gift *par excellence*: *altissimi donum Dei*. Nevertheless secondarily and quite inevitably the supernatural also involves some created gift. This, however, exists only under the aegis of, and in subordination to, the Uncreated Gift. In technical language, reciprocal causalities and priorities are at work here so that the created gift is at once the last disposition for and direct upshot of the advent of the Uncreated; it guarantees the presence of this latter as well as the immediacy of the union between God and man. The new union that is joined when God stoops to give himself to man in friendship exacts, as the price of its own reality, a change somewhere. In God change is unthinkable (Jm 1:17); therefore that change must be located in man (see St. Thomas Aquinas, *Summa contra gentiles* 3, 53, "Amplius ..."). In so far as it is received within man, it partakes of man's finite dimensions and is itself created. It might be described as the footprint of godhead in man caused by the visit of the triune God to man. The interconnection and indissoluble bond between these two "coefficients"—created and Uncreated—has been brilliantly set forth by M. de la Taille [3] and by Karl Rahner.[4] This indissoluble bond explains the compatibility of two streams of tradition about the supernatural: the Greek Fathers of the Church heavily underscored the Uncreated Gift of the in-

---

3. *Recherches de science réligieuse*, 18 (1928), pp. 253-269; *Revue Apologétique* 48 (1929), pp. 5-27, 129-146; *The Incarnation*, Cambridge (1925), pp. 152-190.
4. *Zeitschrift für katholische Theologie* 63 (1939), pp. 137-156.

dwelling Spirit; the post-tridentine theologians on the contrary laid their stress on the created gift of sanctifying grace.
One's view of the supernatural must be broad enough to account for both these accents.

The supernatural, therefore, is a complex reality. When
God decides to take up interpersonal communion with men
he comes with a *cortège* of created gifts that are the signal
and the guarantee of his advent; that abide while he abides;
that prepare and fortify men to bear the stress of the divine
within them and to enter into immediate contact and dialogue
with Father, Son and Holy Spirit.

6) *Three-personed God:* the supernatural is in the highest
degree personal; it involves a dynamic I-Thou encounter.
Father, Son and Holy Spirit, each divine Person comes in his
own reality so that man might cultivate a distinct attitude
and reverent familiarity with each member of the Blessed
Trinity. As a son he turns to the Father; as a brother to the
Son; to the Holy Spirit, indwelling Giver of life, light and
love, he appeals out of his sense of need.

7) *Love and friendship:* this phrase underscores the salient
difference marking off God's presence in the supernatural,
from his omnipresence in the natural order. By very title of
Creator God is everywhere, in the inorganic as well as in the
organic worlds, in the sinner as well as in the saint, in hell
as well as in heaven, in the damned as well as in the elect. By
contrast the supernatural belongs to another sphere and
climate: that of charity and friendship. And because the
Friend and Lover in question is almighty, the new union
and friendship which he establishes between himself and the
creature can never be pegged down to the affective, intentional
order alone. It is much more than wishful thinking. It is real,
ontological and existential—and the guarantee of its reality lies

in the created endowment that is an integral part of the supernatural.

8) Since the supernatural is wrapped in the mystery of Christ
and the Church, it bears the mark of Christ precisely as
Savior and Redeemer. It implies, therefore, that we are sinners
in need of pardon. The unheard of miracle of God's self-
gift to man out of personal love is addressed to a being
stricken with a twofold unworthiness: that of sinner besides
that of creature. Before raising man to the divine the supernatural must first cast down the barrier of sin. This, however,
is not so much a separate, negative process as the reverse side
of the almighty, re-creative act of justification that is norma-
tively accomplished at baptism received in faith. Thus the
supernatural appears as paradoxical: it is at once both sovereignly gratuitous (because intrinsically divine) and stringently
indispensable (because, according to God's decree, necessary
for the remission of sins).

9) The supernatural, carrying God's overtures of personal
love and friendship, calls for man's individual response. Addressed to a being capable of choice and friendship, it chal-
lenges his freedom and seeks to elicit from him an option:
the surrender, the obedience of faith, a *yes* to God's invitation,
a personal and irrevocable engagement. The assent and surrender given to God must be translated into the practice of
daily living. The supernaturalized man must live as befits an
adoptive son of God always mindful of his eternal destiny and
inheritance.

Where is the supernatural to be found?

I) Certainly in the Church, Christ's mystical body whose soul
is the Holy Spirit, Christ continued down the avenues of
history, the treasure-house of all redemptive grace and the

ark of salvation. The visible Church on earth is in vital fellowship with the Church triumphant in heaven. Together they
form the Communion of Saints and the holy People of God and
are full of the supernatural.

II) Supernatural must be applied particularly to the Liturgy
of the Church where she exercises her most lofty function—that
of continuing the priesthood of Christ. The Mass and the
Sacraments (structural elements of the Church), because
they bring us Christ and his Spirit, are definitely supernatural.
Vatican II is our warrant that they carry Christ:

> Christ is always present in His Church, especially in her
> liturgical celebrations. He is present in the sacrifice of the
> Mass, not only in the person of his minister, "the same
> one now offering, through the ministry of priests, who
> formerly offered himself on the cross," but especially under
> the Eucharistic species. By His power He is present in
> the sacraments, so that when a man baptizes it is really
> Christ Himself who baptizes. He is present in His word,
> since it is He Himself who speaks when the holy Scriptures
> are read in the Church. He is present, finally, when the
> Church prays and sings, for He promised: "Where two or
> three are gathered together for my sake, there am I in the
> midst of them" (Mt 18:20). (*Sacrosanctum Concilium* 7,
> Abbott, pp. 140-141).

III) Supernatural *par excellence* will be the beyond-the-tomb
consummation, the absolute *eschaton*. From all generations and
ethnic cultures the scattered children of the heavenly Father
will be gathered with the risen Lord in a community of unending felicity.

IV) As child to man or bud to blossom, so deification on earth
is organically united to or moving towards the beatific vision
in heaven. It is therefore supernatural. Grace-life here is

the ontological prerequisite for glory hereafter. If heaven is to be our authentic fatherland when we shall claim Christ as our Father and share his inheritance (cf. Rm 8:14-1S) we need first to be adoptive children—but that is precisely what justification gives here; that is the meaning of deification and the grace-life on earth: the Holy Spirit resides in us and created grace is poured into our hearts. Any man (Christian or non-Christian) will be able to see God face to face in heaven, if already on earth he has led a life of such unselfishness as evinces his possession of the Holy Spirit, Guest of his soul: *dulcis hospes animae.*

V) Assuredly revelation is supernatural for through it "the invisible God out of the abundance of His love speaks to men as friends" showing forth and communicating "Himself and the eternal decisions of His will" regarding their salvation.[5] Correlative and coupled with this Uncreated Gift of revelation is the created gift of faith in man, for "if this faith is to be shown, the grace of God and the interior help of the Holy Spirit must precede and assist, moving the heart and turning it to God, opening the eyes of the mind, and giving 'joy and ease to everyone in assenting to the truth and believing it.'"[6]

VI) The sacramental characters of baptism, confirmation and orders (as they have been traditionally presented in scholastic theology) are supernatural because they link us with Christ the High Priest, give basic membership or higher status in the Church, and are the point of contact between the Holy Spirit as Soul of the Mystical Body and each individual cell of that Body.[7]

5. Cf. Vatican II, *Dei Verbum* 2 & 6, Abbott, pp. 112 & 114.
6. *Ibid.,* 5, p. 114.
7. See *The Heythrop Journal,* 2, (1961), pp. 318-333.

VII) Internal actual graces of illumination to the mind or inspiration to the will are clearly supernatural when given to one who is already an adoptive son of the heavenly Father. But they are likewise supernatural when they are given to an unbeliever or mortal sinner leading to conversion. They are then best conceived as a fleeting visitation of God to the soul, motivated by the desire for intimate friendship.[8] This indeed is significantly adumbrated in Rv 3:20 through the imagery of the meal shared in common.[9]

VIII) Is Christ himself supernatural? He is the source of all our redemptive supernatural grace and the author of salvation—in that sense he is eminently supernatural. On the other hand, in Christ the three-personed God did not descend to a human *person;* rather the second divine Person assumed a human *nature.* In that sense the supernatural as we define it is not realized in Christ. In a similar way God himself is not supernatural, but the absolute source of his own self-giving to man.

In the following chapters, clarity will benefit if we always keep before our mind the following distinctions: i) the supernatural in itself, in its content, in its objective, historic, extra-mental reality; ii) our concept of it; iii) our technical term for it. There may be divergencies among these three. Thus the supernatural in itself may be much richer than the average Christian thinks it to be. The technical term can be more or less precise, wider or narrower in scope, according to the prevailing theological fashions. The eighteenth century, with its penchant for individualism and abstraction in theology, threw the ecclesial dimension of the supernatural into eclipse.

8. See *Theological Studies*, 8 (1947), pp. 445-471.
9. See *American Ecclesiastical Review* 146 (1962), pp. 47-57.

Parallels appear elsewhere: the nebulous concept of electricity in the mind of an uneducated man hardly squares with the reality; and the word itself may convey differing shades of meaning for the popular writer, the expert in electro-dynamics or the lexicographer. Similarly, the Latin *sacramentum* has, in the course of its history, run through the gamut of many meanings. But sacraments, as divinely appointed, structural elements of the Church have been there from the start, though not till the later Middle Ages did the technical term take shape. Even today this is more or less satisfactory according as one acknowledges the ecclesial aspect or reduces the sacrament to being simply *signum efficax gratiae.*

We claim that our definition of the supernatural represents the technical term in its most ample and adequate sense; that this, in its turn, matches a concept of the supernatural that is drawn from and mirrors the whole, objective reality. Others have other concepts and read less into the technical term. The discussions that ensue must be the explanation and justification of our usage.

Chapter 2

EARLY scholasticism may be taken as beginning with St. Anselm of Canterbury (c. 1033-1109), often called its father. It includes, among many others, such writers as Anselm of Laon (ob. 1117), Hugo of Saint-Victor (ob. 1141), Abelard (ob. 1142), William of Saint-Thierry (ob. 1148), St. Bernard of Clairvaux (ob. 1153), Gilbert de la Porrée (ob. 1154: the more thoroughly historians of dogma investigate early scholasticism the more clearly Gilbert's influence emerges), Peter Lombard (ob. 1160: his book of *Sentences* became the textbook of predilection for subsequent medieval theologians, including St. Thomas). Early scholasticism closes with Philip the Chancellor (ob. 1236: a masterly and original thinker whose chief work, *Summa de bono*, still remains in manuscript in the Vatican Library: cod. Vat. Lat. 7669).

Difficult assessment

It is hard for us moderns to gain an exact and undistorted understanding of the teaching of the early scholastics on any given dogmatic theme—and this especially for two reasons. First, we westerners are willy-nilly heirs to scholasticism such as it was canonized by the Council of Trent and refined and elaborated by the labors of the post-tridentine theologians. Hence we tend to read back into these earlier treatises our nineteenth and twentieth century clear-cut, technical concepts. Impulsively we seek to illuminate the dark patches of early scholasticism with the light acquired across many centuries of theological probing and sophistication. To yield to this impulse would be to falsify and to misinterpret. For what appears to us dark in the writings of that age might well have been in fact dark to the thinkers of the time. Inevitably at its dawning scholasticism was everywhere obscure and inchoate. Nowhere did it achieve systematic coherence and definitive clarification. Thus Anselm of Canterbury gave the first great impulse to speculations on the nature of sin and its relationship to divine causality.[1] But in handling this intricate question, the early scholastics, despite their skill in dialectics, were unable to reach a satisfactory solution through a downright lack of metaphysical equipment. Their discussions, though notably meritorious in the case of Gilbert de la Porrée and his school, became stricken with sterility from which they were freed by St. Bonaventure with some help from Aristotelic metaphysics. Naturally, then, we shall expect that early scholasticism will furnish us with a concept of the supernatural at many points poorer than what we find at its heyday. Unless we admit this we can scarcely claim that we acknowledge a development of dogma.

Secondly, a problem quite special to early scholasticism confronts the modern investigator; most of the material still remains hidden away in manuscript. From a vast corpus of

1. *De conceptu virginali et de originali peccato,* cap. 4, *Opera Omnia,* ed. Schmitt, vol. 2, Rome (1940), p. 143.

writing relatively little has been published. Hence (as Cardinal Ehrle pointed out nearly fifty years ago) any judgment relying solely on the published works of those early authors risks being of little or of quite ephemeral value. How then is one to cope with this jungle of manuscript literature? Luckily in recent years (from 1952 onwards) the indispensable and monumental volumes of A. M. Landgraf have appeared: *Dogmengeschichte der Frühscholastik*, Regensburg. In these, with massive erudition and highminded objectivity, Landgraf draws copiously on both published and manuscript sources. Hence we shall lean heavily on him, as well as on Z. Alszeghy [2] who provides a masterly bibliographical survey.

The setting of early scholasticism

The theological exchanges of the early scholastics were mostly conducted in a calm and peaceful spirit. There were indeed prominent exceptions—plently of *furor theologicus* was fanned up around the names of Gerhoh of Reichersberg (ob. 1169), Walter of St. Victor (ob. *c.* 1190) and Abelard. In general, however, scholasticism enjoyed a serene and tranquil dawning. Characteristic of these early scholastics was the tenacity of their pursuit of a question once broached until a solution had been found or the matter exhausted. The endless minutiae of their painstaking thrashing out of a problem make tedious reading. One might check this by following the ins and outs of their discussion on charity and temptation.[3]

A grave handicap of early scholasticism, especially apropos of the supernatural, was its ignorance of Semipelagianism—

2. "La teologia dell'ordine soprannaturale nella scolastica antica," *Gregorianum* 31 (1950), pp. 414-450.

3. Cf. Landgraf, *op. cit.*, "Caritas und Widerstand gegen die Versuchungen," (1953), 1/2, chapter 5.

which underwent a long theological eclipse from 900 till 1271.
St. Thomas, by about 1265 when he came to compose his
Summa Theologica (but not much before), had rediscovered
the semipelagian error and the *initium fidei*, not in the
second council of Orange (which remained in oblivion till
about 1500) but in the works of St. Augustine.[4]

The early scholastics did not speculate for speculation's
sake. They were men of faith who started from the revealed
message as found in Sacred Scripture. They expounded the
text and sought to grasp its meaning, raising questions and
attempting to reconcile apparent contradictions: *fides quaerens
intellectum.* They took it for granted that every intelligent
Christian wanted to understand his faith. "Faith," wrote William of Saint-Thierry, "because it's an affair of knowledge,
quite spontaneously seeks to know whatever is proposed for
belief" (*fides, quia scientiae res est, quasi naturaliter scire
appetit, quidquid ei credendum indicitur, Speculum fidei*
PL 180. 387. A). He held up Our Lady as the model of the
enquiring mind (*vide matrem Domini, speciale fidei signum,
ibid.,* 381. C). Most firmly she believed Gabriel's message that
she was to be the mother of the Lord. Nevertheless she
wanted to understand the *how* of this mystery. Hence her
quomodo fiet istud? Likewise the thinking Christian will want
to moot questions about the faith which he holds: *Quomodo
fiunt ista?* Quite right, says William, provided that his queries
be a prayer, an expression of love, filial reverence and of
modest seeking (*quaestio tua, oratio tua sit, amor sit, pietas
sit, et humile desiderium, ibid.* 384. B). It was in such a
spirit and in such an atmosphere that these thinkers slowly
and tentatively worked out a theology of the supernatural—

4. See: H. Bouillard, *Conversion et grâce chez S. Thomas d'Aquin,*
Paris (1944), especially pp. 92-123. Also M. Seckler, *Instinkt und
Glaubenswille nach Thomas von Aquin,* Mainz (1961), pp. 90-170.

which, however, up till about the first quarter of the thirteenth
century remained largely inadequate.

Lack of technical terminology

In order to appraise the early scholastic teaching on the
supernatural, the obvious course is to search out what these
writers express about *supernaturale*. However any such direct
proceeding is barred by the fact that nowhere, when discussing man's deification, do the early scholastics use *supernaturale*
unequivocally in its technical sense.[5] Hence it is necessary
to take a roundabout way. One gradually pieces together
their theology of the supernatural by examining what these
early scholastic thinkers offer on such headings as Pelagianism,
grace, virtue, merit, faith, charity, sin and the fall, justification
and the preparation for it. Naturally the conclusion emerges
that their theology of the supernatural lacked maturity and
completeness. Its deficiencies sprang from such factors as the
fluidity of terminology, the lack of clear and distinct ideas, in-
sufficient metaphysics, an excessive attention to the relative,
moral-psychological, as against the absolute, ontological necessity of grace. Briefly, the early scholastics thought too much
about *gratia sanans* and too little about *gratia elevans*. Of
course with the passing of time their theology of the supernatural matured until with Philip the Chancellor it reached
the verge of being a coherently thought out system.[6] Some
closer inspection is desirable here.

The early scholastic theology of the supernatural took

5. Landgraf is emphatic here: "Die Tatsache lässt sich nicht best-
reiten, dass im Zusammenhang mit der Gnadenlehre das Wort *super-*
naturale bis zum Beginn des 13. Jahrhunderts nicht ein einzigesmal an
entscheidender Stelle auftritt," *op. cit.*, 1/1, p. 141.
6. Landgraf, *op. cit.*, 1/1, pp. 201, 214-219.

its rise from St. Paul with his insistence on the gratuity of
justification. Pauline commentaries formed the cradle of
scholasticism. St. Augustine contributed the terminology: *gratia operans, cooperans, adiutrix, adiuvans, auxiliatrix, praeveniens, praeventrix, subsequens, aspirans, suscitans, comi-
tans, consummans, conservatrix, incipiens, perseverans, sub-
levans.* Now in the twelfth century, none of these expressions
denoted what most of them would immediately convey to
the modern scholastic theologian—i.e., actual as opposed to
habitual grace. All of them signified abiding, justifying
grace.[7] It was not until the beginning of the thirteenth century
that a grace other than justifying was described as *excitans*
or *praeparans.* Early scholastic terminology was varied and
flexible. *Gratia* might refer to charity or faith; *gratia cooperans*
might be employed for virtue; both *gratia operans* and *gratia
gratis dans* sometimes meant God himself.[8] *Datum, donum,
gratuitum* were used with considerable looseness.

Shortage of distinctions

However this absence of a fixed, clear-cut technical terminology in early scholasticism constituted perhaps no serious
obstacle. Even fully-fledged and systematized theologies can
support both growth and reasonable latitude here. Measured
against a full-blossomed scholasticism, a graver defect was
the failure or slowness to distinguish what needed distinguish-
ing. Thus, actual was not marked off from habitual grace.
Justifying grace was not divided from faith and charity.
These two virtues, in their turn, were not sorted out from
one another and from their acts. So much did the early
scholastics think of the grace needed to elicit God-pleasing

7. *Ibid.*, pp. 51-52.
8. *Ibid.*, pp. 127-129.

acts in terms of virtue that, conversely, they were embarrassed over the situation of baptized babies, precisely because these are incapable of eliciting acts of faith, hope and charity.[9] Likewise, in early scholasticism, acquired and infused virtues, "informed" and "uninformed" faith were originally lumped together. The concepts of goodness, merit and gratuity were ill-defined and merging. It was confrontation with Pelagianism that forced the early scholastics to discriminate between the gifts of nature and of grace. As we remarked, the root weakness of early scholasticism was its failure to underscore the vital difference between healing and elevating grace. This failure itself was especially due to a concentration on man's fall and not on the transcendence of his end. To construct an adequate theology of the supernatural, the *point de départ* must be the beatific vision: the absolute need of elevating, proportioning grace springs from the magnificence of this goal. The early scholastics, by focussing on man's beginning and his fall, were constrained to cut down the concept of grace to little else than God's remedial intervention.

Original sin

Early scholasticism looked on original sin as a disturbance of nature, as physical damage inflicted on man, dislocating his thinking and willing. Through the fall the alignment (so to speak) of mind and will went awry.[10] The early scholastics asked the question: "how can man, wounded by original sin, possibly lead a decent Christian life?" They answered: "grace." The very context of their preoccupations led them to narrow

9. This embarrassment is reflected in St. Anselm of Canterbury's *De conceptu virginali et de originali peccato,* chapter 29, Schmitt, pp. 172-173.

10. Landgraf, *op. cit.,* 1/1, pp. 99-114.

the scope of grace to a restoration of man's psychological bal-
ance and health; to the healing of his nature so that it might
once more enjoy its primeval resilience and competence; to
the endowing of him once more with justice—presented by
St. Anselm in wholly moralist or voluntarist terminology.[11]
Since the wounding of human nature by original sin found
its most concrete expression in the damage done to the intellect
and will, the rehabilitating process of justification was cor-
respondingly seen by the early scholastics as a re-orientation
of the intellect through the lodging in it of faith, and of the
will through that of charity. When, however, one thus restricts
grace to a divine patching up of wounded nature or to a
redressing of man's psychological incapacity or to a bolster-
ing of his moral feebleness one remains at a far cry from the
full reality of the supernatural: inward transformation of man,
ontological raising of him to a divine level of existence; self-
communication of the three-personed God out of personal
love.

Interrelated terms

We moderns shall be able to assess more justly early
scholastic theology of the supernatural if we understand
more accurately the key vocabulary employed:—grace and
gratuitousness; merit and goodness; faith and charity. In
early scholasticism these terms are closely interrelated; often
one is best understood in function of the other.
Inspired by St. Paul (Rm 3:24; 11:6) and St. Augustine
(*Spir. et litt.* 10. 16), Peter Lombard had launched into circula-

11. *Rectitudo voluntatis propter se servata*, e.g., *De libertate arbitrii*,
chapters 3 & 13; Schmitt I, pp. 212, lines 22-23 & 225, line 10;
De conceptu virginali et de originali peccato, chapters 3 & 5, Schmitt
II, p. 143, lines 7 & 147, line 1.

tion the concept of grace as a gift unowed to human endeavor which all early scholastic speculation on this matter endorsed.[12] Grace was defined in function of its gratuity. Its character of being what cannot be humanly merited was treated as its essence.[13]

Grace, then, was coupled with the gratuitous which itself acquired in early scholasticism the quasi-technical significance of being what was beyond the reach of human merit, or what was conferred on man by God from sheer bounty.[14] At the time of Peter Lombard man's substance and faculties (memory, intellect, will) were commonly labelled *naturalia;* the *gratuita* were the endowments bounteously added by God to nature: *naturalibus superadiecta sunt . . . a Deo homini per gratiam conferuntur.*[15]

Early scholasticism defined grace and gratuity as that which transcends the grasp of purely human work, struggle and desert, as that which, therefore, cannot be claimed by any of these. How did it understand *merit* properly so called, theological merit—that quality in a work that gives it currency with God and entitles the worker to a reward? Early scholasticism of course recognized the necessity of man's free will. We are not concerned with this, but rather with its attitude to the requirement of grace for supernatural merit. In fact early scholasticism took as normative and axiomatic for all its thinking on merit the words of St. Augustine which are enshrined in the *Indiculus* (Denz 248):

12. Landgraf, *op. cit.,* 1/1, pp. 148-161.
13. . . . "die Unverdienbarkeit als Wesen der Gnade . . ." *ibid.,* p. 149.
14. Master Martin writes: *". . . dicuntur gratuita, quia homini conferuntur sine meritis humanis ex sola gratia"* quoted by Landgraf, *op. cit.,* 1/1, p. 157.
15. *Ibid.*

Tanta est erga homines boni-tas Dei, ut nostra velit esse merita, quae sunt ipsius dona (Epist. 194, 5, 19; *In evang. Ioh.* 3, 10; *Corrept.* 13, 41).

The goodness of God towards men is so great that he wishes to be our merits what in fact are his own gifts (see Land-graf, *op. cit.*, 1/1, pp. 183-201; 1/2, pp. 75-110).

Merit, therefore, flows from God's initiative and love. Only after God has first intervened conferring charity on man can there be, for the early scholastics, any question of merit. God-given charity dominates their concept of merit and is its source. They thought of merit exclusively in the context of charity. This means that for them all merit is what later theology christened *condign.* This does *not* mean that they necessarily denied the possibility of *congruous* merit—i.e., an action, prior to justification, elicited under the influence of *actual* grace. They simply refused to call such actions meritorious because they reserved this title to merit in the most authentic sense—i.e., actions proceeding from a man in the state of charity. In a similar way, the early scholastics generally ascribed *goodness* only to behavior that is condignly meritorious—therefore to God-pleasing actions elicited by an adoptive child of God.[16]

Charity

Charity, which commands the early scholastic attitude to merit, looms large in all these discussions. The scholastics associated charity intimately with faith which they called the first grace.[17] Faith was understood in its pregnant sense

16. *Ibid.*, 1/1, e.g., p. 108.
17. "radix . . . omnium virtutum, et fundamentum bonorum operum,"

as working through charity (Gal 5:6); and charity, in its turn, was associated with faith. So much are faith and charity intertwined in early scholastic thought that William of Saint-Thierry can write (and his words amount to a definition of faith): belief in Christ is going to him in love (*credere . . . in eum, amando in eum ire est.*[18] *Speculum fidei.* PL 180, 383, B, cf., 371, A . . . *amor Christi sine quo fides in Christum omnino esse non potest*). He insists on this point:

Cur enim non credis, o infidelis? Utique quia non diligis. Non credis, quia non diligis; non diligis, quia non credis. Neque enim alterum esse potest sine altero; quia alterum pendet ex altero. (*Ibid.*, 371, A-B. Cf. 391 A, "*in eis vero quae sunt ad Deum, sensus mentis amor est,*" Déchanet, pp. 68-70 and p. 156).	Unbeliever, why do you not believe? Assuredly because you do not love. You do not believe because you do not love; you do not love, because you do not believe. One cannot exist without the other; they are mutually dependent.

In all these discussions conducted by the early scholastics there is no elaborated theology of the supernatural. The mutual relationship of grace and the virtues, the distinctions between ethical and supernatural goodness, between the gratuity of what subsequent theology would call the preternatural and the entitatively supernatural at first find no place. Once

William of Saint-Thierry, *Speculum fidei*, PL 180, 376 D. In Déchanet's edition (1946), p. 94.

---

18. *Speculum fidei*, PL 180, 383 B; cf. 371 A . . . *amor Christi sine quo fides in Christum omnino esse non potest.*

more there is the failure to appreciate the absolute necessity
of an elevating grace proportioning man to the vision of
God, his final end.

Pelagianism avoided?

The early scholastics use many phrases that to our ears
have a decidedly pelagian ring about them. Sometimes they
speak as though a man can give himself faith without the
help of grace [19] or, when handling the problem of grace and
free will, they effect illustrations that seem to exclude grace [20];
or again they will make play with the axiom: "God does not
withhold his grace from the man who does what lies in his
own power" (*facenti quod est in se Deus non denegat gra-*)
tiam) with a sort of reckless abandon that would make the
hair of the post-tridentine theologian stand on end [21]; or,
lastly, they refer to the acts previous and preparatory to
justification as though they are elicited without any grace
and are bereft of even congruous merit.[22]

To judge all such positions fairly we need to get facts
into historical focus and recall what has already been pointed
out: i.e., that they reserve the name *grace* to justification,
and that they are interested exclusively in condign merit.
Not thinking of actual grace, they should not be accused

19. E.g., William of Saint-Thierry's discussion on the two sorts
of faith, one for the lukewarm, the other for the fervent; one revealed
by flesh and blood, the other by the Father in heaven — *Speculum fidei*,
PL 180, 378-379.

20. E.g., they liken grace to sunlight: a man has it in his own
power to open his eyes or to keep them closed. The implication is
that without grace he is able to consent to grace — Landgraf, *op. cit.*,
1/1, p. 81

21. See Landgraf, *op. cit.*, pp. 249-264.

22. *Ibid.*, pp. 238-302.

of repudiating it. Landgraf's emphatic conclusion after his painstaking investigation of the question certainly carries conviction: in their historical context, these scholastic writings in fact have a thoroughly orthodox sense.[23]

Landgraf's conclusion cannot be seriously challenged if we are prepared soberly to read these early scholastic treatises in the historical perspective of the preoccupations of their authors. We can test this by taking at random three samples: St. Anselm of Canterbury, St. Bernard and William of Saint-Thierry.

St. Anselm: We find in St. Anselm's theology of the supernatural such inadequacies as appertain to all early scholastic thinkers and as were mentioned in a general way above. Thus throughout he lays greater stress on justification as release from the deleterious *sequelae* of original sin than on deification. And he seems more concerned with man's recovery of a likeness to the angels than to God.[24] Elsewhere, however, he leaves no doubt as to God's initiative in man's restoration. No will, he affirms, can have rectitude except as God's gift; and once it has abandoned this God-given rectitude, only God can restore it (. . . *sicut nulla voluntas, antequam haberet rectitudinem, potuit eam deo non dante capere: ita cum deserit acceptam, non potest eam nisi deo reddente recipere*).[25] Especially in his intense and beautifully formulated *orationes*

23. *Ibid.,* 1/1, p. 302: "Aua dem Gesagten dürfte sich ergeben haben, dass in der Frühscholastik tatsächlich Wendungen auftreten, die unseren Ohren pelagianisch klingen, aber zugleich, dass sie innerhalb der Gesamtpartitur des frühscholastichen Theologie gehört, die Harmonie nicht stören und einen durchaus orthodoxen Sinn haben."

24. See *De conceptu virginali* . . . , chapter 28, Schmitt 2, p. 171, line 21; *Meditatio redemptionis humanae,* Schmitt 3, p. 86, line 72.

25. *De libertate arbitrii,* Schmitt I, p. 222, lines 11-13.

sive meditationes do we glimpse the soundness of his under-standing of the supernatural. The primacy of God in the affair of man's salvation is recurringly suggested in a vital, prayed form:

. . . *tu donas si quid bene vult anima mea . . . da quod me facis velle, da ut quantum iubes tantum te merear a-mare . . . Laudes et gratias tibi ago pro desiderio quod in-spirasti* (*Oratio ad Christum,* Schmitt, 3, pp. 6-7, lines 15-18).

. . . it is Your gift, if my soul wants anything well . . . grant what You make me want; grant that I may deserve to love You as much as You want . . . I praise and thank You for the desire You have inspired in me.

. . . *expectat anima mea ad sufficienter paenitendum, ad bene vivendum tuae gratiae inspirationem* (*ibid.,* p. 7, lines 27-28).

. . . in order to repent properly and live rightly my soul a-waits the inpouring of Your grace.

The *Oratio ad sanctam Mariam pro impetrando eius et Christi amore,* so full of rich mariological insights, everywhere pro-claims salvation as God's gift or as coming, under God, through Mary:

Non est enim reconciliatio ni-si quam tu casta concepisti, non est iustificatio nisi quam tu integra in utero fovisti, non est salus nisi quam tu virgo peperisti (*Oratio 7,* Schmitt, 3, p. 23, lines 122-124).

For there is no atonement ex-cept what you have chastely conceived; there is no justi-fication except what you have inviolably cherished in your womb; there is no salvation except what you have vir-ginally brought forth.

In his *Oratio ad accipiendum corpus domini et sanguinem*

Anselm begs that through the Eucharist he might be formed
to the likeness of Christ's death and resurrection by a mortify-
ing of the old man and newness of a life of justice—that so
he might be worthy to be incorporated into Christ's body
"which is the Church" and so might be a member of Christ,
with Christ as his Head, with Christ remaining in him and he
in Christ.[26] One has here by implication and in *résumé* the
whole of the supernatural.

Finally we have Anselm's *Meditatio redemptionis humanae*,
an epitome of his classic work *Cur Deus homo?* and a gem
of spirituality.

Christianum me fecisti vocari de nomine tuo, per quod et ego confiteor et tu cognoscis me inter redemptos tuos; et erexisti et levasti me ad notitiam et amorem tuum... (*Meditatio* 3, Schmitt, 3, p. 90, lines 184-186).

You have made me a Chris-
tian to be called by Your
name, whereby both I pro-
claim myself and You ac-
knowledge me to be amongst
Your redeemed; and you have
raised and lifted me up to
the knowledge and love of
You ...

A te habeo desiderare, a te habeam impetrare... (*ibid.,* p. 91, lines 206-207).

From You I have my desire;
may I have from You the
granting of my request.

Such passages as these (and there are many similar) leave
no doubt as to Anselm's incontestable orthodoxy. They witness besides to his profound penetration into the mystery of
the supernatural.

St. Bernard: The authentic mystics of Christianity can shed
much light on our understanding of the supernatural. For they

26. *Oratio* III, Schmitt, p. 10, lines 15-19.

have a personal and direct approach, an experiential contact with it—of particular value in an age when the supernatural was studied moralistically, under the aspect of *gratia sanans* rather than *elevans*. Besides being a theologian, Bernard is a saint and a mystic as well. In his treatise *De gratia et libero arbitrio* where he addresses himself to the perplexing problem of grace and free will, he makes it plain that salvation comes from God, though of course man must respond to God's overtures:

Deus auctor salutis est, liberum arbitrium tantum capax: nec dare illam nisi Deus, nec capere valet nisi liberum arbitrium. Quod ergo a solo Deo et soli datur libero arbitrio, tam absque consensu esse non potest accipientis, quam absque gratia dantis. (*De gratia et libero arbitrio*, 4; *Sancti Bernardi Opera*, Rome, 1963, vol. 3, p. 166, lines 22-25).

God is the author of salvation, only the free will is capable of being saved: only God can give salvation, only the free will is able to receive it. Therefore what is given by God alone to the free will alone can neither be without the consent of the receiver nor the grace of the giver.

In his *De diligendo Deo* Bernard insists on God's initiative in loving [27] and that this prevenient divine love (... *Maiestas in amore praeveniens, tota in opus salutis... intensa*) calls for our love in return.[28] He points out how in creating us God gave us ourselves and in redeeming us he gave us himself and so restored us to ourselves (*In primo opere me mihi dedit, in secundo se; et ubi se dedit, me mihi reddidit*).[29] God,

27. 1, 1 *Opera*, vol. 3, pp. 120-121.
28. *Ibid.*, 4, 13; p. 130, lines 5-14.
29. *Ibid.*, 5, 15; p. 132, lines 10-11.

he explains, rewards us for loving him, but charity is disinterested; we must not bargain with God; charity is love, not a juridical pact (*affectus est, non contractus*).[30] It comes from God who is charity:

Dicitur ergo recte caritas, et Deus, et Dei donum. Itaque caritas dat caritatem, substantiva accidentalem. Ubi dantem significat, nomen substantiae est; ubi donum, qualitatis (Opera, 12, 35, p. 149, lines 26-28).	Therefore charity is rightly called both God and the gift of God. Thus charity gives charity, substantial gives accidental. When charity refers to the giver it names a substance; when it refers to the gift, it names a quality.

Bernard exhorts his readers to a wholehearted surrender to God, shutting out all thought of personal gain. For him this is what deification in the concrete should mean: total, unstinted commitment to the Lord: *sic affici, deificari est.*[31] These rapid indications may suffice to show that St. Bernard understood and proclaimed salient features of the supernatural.

William of Saint-Thierry: Like St. Bernard, to whom he was deeply devoted, Abbot William drew his inspiration from the Scriptures. He was very much aware of the joy of personal contact with God found in a faith translated into the practice of daily living (*dulcis accessus, bonae conscientiae suavitas ... suavitas experientiae*).[32] This sweetness arising from union with God is a favorite theme of William.[33] He expects Christian faith to be mature and intelligent and shows himself very sensitive to difficulties that beset Christians against faith.

30. *Ibid.*, 7, 17; p. 133, line 23.
31. *Ibid.*, 10, 28; p. 143, line 15.
32. *Speculum fidei*, PL 180, 394 B; cf. *ibid.*, 382 B: ". . . *parti-*

Judging William by more recent standards, one might point
to certain infelicities of expression in his theology of faith.
But on the primacy and initiative of God in faith and in
everything supernatural one cannot fault him. For him faith
is a work of the Holy Spirit (*operante Spiritu sancto*, PL 180,
376 A—see 386 C: *nec . . . nisi Deo dante . . .*) requiring the
aid of God's grace (*nec sine magno auxilio gratiae Dei effici
potest—ibid.*, 376 B—see 388 C). Grace plays the role of
nursing mother, the will that of daughter (*agnosce matrem
gratiam . . . voluntas vero in hoc filia gratiae est. Gratia gene-
rat, gratia lactat, gratia nutrit ac provehit, et ad perfectum
usque perducit—*371 C-D). He heavily underscores the illumi-
nating character of faith, employing *gratia illuminans* almost
a dozen times in his *Speculum fidei*. As with his contemporaries, so with him—the interest centers on faith working
through charity—implying, therefore, adoptive sonship,[34] the
presence of Christ in our hearts,[35] the indwelling Spirit,[36] the
interior Deus who shares in human nature so as to give
us a share in his godhead (*ad hoc inclinaverat se ad consortium humanitatis nostrae, ut participes nos efficeret divinitatis suae—*PL, 180, 382, C). Because William sees so clearly
the supernaturality of faith therefore he insists on prayer that
God might grant growth and stability (*ibid.*, 378, A; 388, B).

He is emphatic on the fact that all charity begins with

ceps . . . eius suavitatis."

33. See: *suavitas, suavis, suaviter* in "table des mots latins" in
M. M. Davy's edition of William's works, Paris (1953 & 1959). See also
De natura et dignitate amoris, nn. 35-37; Davy, pp. 112-116.

————————

34. 371 B, see *De contemplando Deo*, ed. Davy, (1953), pp. 54-56,
nn. 19 & 20.

35. PL 180, 371 C, 379 C.

36. *Ibid.*, 373 A; Davy, *op. cit.*, p. 52, n. 18.

God's action, comes from him and is addressed to him:

amore tuo provocans et suscitans ad te amorem nostrum...

with your love calling forth and prompting our love for you (*De contempl. Deo*, 17, Davy, p. 52—see 16, p. 50. Also *De natura et dignitate amoris*, 5, Davy, pp. 74-76).

Amor illuminatus caritas est: amor a Deo, in Deo, ad Deum caritas est... Quicquid de Deo dici potest, potest dici et de caritate; sic tamen ut, considerata secundum naturas doni et dantis, in dante nomen sit substantiae, in dato qualitatis (De natura et dignitate amoris, 15, Davy, p. 88).

Enlightened love is charity. Charity is love from God, in God, towards God. Whatever can be said about God can also be said about charity—with this proviso that, when charity is compared according to the reality of gift and giver, it names a substance in the giver, and a quality in the gift.

(The concluding phrase, which we saw paralleled in Bernard *supra*, reminds us that this contemplative is also a scholastic theologian).

A final quotation from William:

Festina ergo particeps esse Spiritus sancti. Adest cum invocatur; nec nisi iam adsit, invocatur. Cumque invocatus venit, in abundantia venit benedictionis Dei... Ipse est lumen illuminans; ipse trahens caritas; ipse afficiens suavitas;

Hasten then to be a sharer in the Holy Spirit. When He is addressed He is present; nor is He addressed unless already present. When He comes because He has been addressed, He comes in the plenitude of God's blessing... He Himself

| *ipse hominis ad Deum acces-* *sus; ipse amor amantis.* | is light which sheds light, charity which draws, sweetness which touches, man's bridge to God, the love of the Lover. |

(*Speculum fidei*, PL, 180, 384, B and D. See concluding apostrophe of *De contempl. Deo.* 28, Davy, pp. 64-66. It is noteworthy that William speaks of the Church as the Mystical Body and of our sharing the divine life of the Head—*De nat. et dignitate amoris*, 35-37, Davy, pp. 112-116.)

Given the evolving state of theology in William's age, one wonders whether he could possibly have shown greater awareness of the supernatural than he displays in his writings.

Chapter 3

SUPERNATURAL IN HIGH (13TH CENTURY) SCHOLASTICISM

THE handiest way of arriving at an appreciation of the theology of the supernatural in high scholasticism is to concentrate chiefly on its most illustrious spokesman St. Thomas Aquinas (1225–1274). He stands in the debt of his predecessors, the early scholastics in general and of his master St. Albert the Great in particular. His thought is continuous with theirs. His theology is not his own invention, but an organic growth from theirs. However, instead of their inevitable fumblings, obscurities and incompleteness, he displays serene assurance and exceptional clarity. What he has inherited from them has been worked on by his own genius. A striking illustration of St. Thomas' conciseness and mastery is his treatment, within the small compass of a single article, of the preparation for justification.[1] By contrast, Landgraf (*Dogmengeschichte der Frühscholastik* 1/1 chapter 8) records, *per longum ac latum,* the gropings and indecisiveness of the early scholastics dealing with the same theme.

1. ST 1a, 2ae, 109.6; also *ibid.,* 112.2 & 3.

To do full justice to St. Thomas' theology of the supernatural would require the handling of a large array of topics.
For example, the swing in his thinking as one moves from
his earlier to his later writings; or the contribution of his
exegetical as against his dogmatic works.[2] One would need
to investigate his Christology, especially his doctrine of the
Redemption. One would need to remember the cosmic, salvific dimension he discerns in Mary's consent at the Annunci-
ation.[3] Again, St. Thomas' emphasis on the supernaturality
of faith[4] is an important aspect of his general theology of
the supernatural. His teaching on the communitarian side
of the supernatural could be gathered from his studies on the
sacraments (especially Eucharist and Baptism) and on the
Church as the Mystical Body of Christ.[5] The fact that the
supernatural lodges in us dynamic gifts that constitute a summons to the apostolate and service of our fellows is suggested
by St. Thomas when he deals with Confirmation (ST 3a, 72,
5).

If St. Thomas splendidly safeguards the gratuity and transcendence of the supernatural, he likewise has penetrating
statements on the correlative aspect of immanence: i.e., man's

2. His commentary on *Romans* is particularly rich and important.
One thinks of such packed paragraphs as *In Rom.* 4:1 or 8:3, Marietti
(1953), par. 325 & 647. In parenthesis, the commentary on John is
very clear on divine initiative — *In Joan.* 15:3 and on our absolute need
of Christ: 15:1.

3. See Leo XIII's comment on ST 3a, 30.1; Denz 3321.

4. This has been magisterially treated by R. Aubert, *Le problème
de l'acte de foi* (1950), pp. 43-71 with copious references. But see
also M. Seckler, *Instinkt und Glaubenwille,* Mainz (1961), with E.
Schillebeeckx, *Concept of Truth and Theological Renewal,* London
(1968), pp. 30-75.

5. St. Thomas interprets the allegory of the vine in an ecclesial
sense. Christ, he writes, is *vitis vera secundum hoc quod est caput Ec-
clesiae, In Joan.* 15:1.

yearning for the supernatural. We touch here on the hotly controverted issues connected with the natural desire of the beatific vision over which oceans of ink have been spilt.[6] In whatever sense these stormy problems are solved we must recognize that St. Thomas taught such a natural desire *at least* in the way Augustine also did: "You have made us for yourself, Lord, and restless is our heart until it rests in you" (*Conf.* 1, 1).

These then are some of the topics whose discussion would enable us to fill in the picture of St. Thomas on the supernatural. In fact requirements of space force us to resign ourselves to a much more modest program. Our aim is merely to offer a rapid and decidedly limited assessment of St. Thomas' theology of the supernatural by considering only the following four headings: (I) word, (II) last end, (III) created grace and (IV) participation.

(*I*) *The word supernatural:* In chapter 6 we shall have more to report about the history of this key term of scholastic theology. For the moment we wish merely to draw attention to a fact of history: St. Thomas stands out above all others as deserving most credit for shaping *supernatural* into a technical term of the first importance and for ensuring its circulation in the theology of the West.

(*II*) *Last End:* The superiority of high scholastic theology of the supernatural over early scholasticism is that the former is shaped by a consideration of man's last end: the beatific vision. The early scholastics (following St. Augustine) concentrated on man's fall and thus inferred his need of *healing*

6. See G. Colombo, "Il problema del soprannaturale negli ultimi cinquant'anni," *Problemi e orientamenti di teologia dommatica,* vol. 2 (1957), pp. 546-607 with bibliography.

grace. While allowing for this procedure, St. Thomas preferred to shift the accent and to spotlight the transcendence of man's end. He thus easily deduces the absolute necessity of *elevating* grace. Both healing and elevating grace fit harmoniously into his scheme. For right living in the fullest sense, man needs (he teaches):

aliquod habituale donum, per quod natura humana corrupta sanetur, et etiam sanata elevetur ad operanda opera meritoria vitae aeternae quae excedunt proportionem naturae (ST 1a, 2ae, 109, 9)

some abiding gift, whereby human nature, spoilt through sin, is healed and also, once healed, is raised to elicit acts meritorious of life everlasting, which are beyond the reach of nature.

St. Thomas has expressed his insight into the commanding importance of the end in the following memorable and incisive words:

...homo post peccatum ad plura indiget gratia quam ante peccatum, sed non magis; quia homo etiam ante peccatum indigebat gratia ad vitam aeternam consequendam, quae est principalis necessitas gratiae (ST 1a, 95, 4, ad 1).

...after sin man needs grace for more purposes than before sin, but he does not have a greater need of it; for even before sin man needed grace to gain everlasting life—and this is the chief need for grace.

To solve the problems connected with the supernatural, with a sort of relentless lucidity St. Thomas keeps on swinging back to the nature of man's goal. Thus when the question is raised: "can a man merit life everlasting without grace?" he answers by formulating this principle: between the end and what is geared to it there must be intrinsic proportioning

(... *actus perducentes ad finem oportet esse fini proportionatos*
—ST 1a, 2ae, 109.5) or again: "which is better—sanctifying
grace or a charism like prophecy or wonder-working?" St.
Thomas replies—"the former, because it directly links a man
with his last end (... *ordinat hominem immediate ad con-
iunctionem ultimi finis*). Charisms effect this link only indirectly" (ST 1a, 2ae, 111.5). In other words, the end commands everything else. A glance at the index of the book III of
the *Summa contra Gentiles* shows how highly developed is
Thomas' theology of the beatific vision—in marked contrast
with the embryonic stage of its growth in early scholasticism.
With St. Thomas the thought of the end might almost be
described as obsessive. His theology is at once teleological and
eschatological—hence its strength and coherence.

St. Thomas' doctrine of supernatural life on earth as the
inchoatio formalis gloriae is a convincing illustration of the
tightly-knit, interlocking nature of his system and (once
again) of the pre-eminent importance of man's last end.
Basing himself on the Scriptures (e.g., Jn 3:16; 17:3; 1 Cor
13:9-13) St. Thomas teaches that already here on earth, in
the believer, glory is begun. Here is the dawning of that day
whose noon-tide is the beatific vision. Thus faith is not only
the beginning and, as it were, the groundwork of the entire
supernatural life (*prima inchoatio et fundamentum quoddam
quasi totius spiritualis vitae—De ver.* 14.2 ad 1), it is more
specifically "a kind of beginning of everlasting life, which
we hope for from the divine promise" (*ibid., in corpore*).
Elsewhere he describes it as a *foretaste* of that bliss and
knowledge to come which we will have *in patria* (*praelibatio
illius futurae beatitudinis et cognitionis quam habebimus in
patria—In Joan.* 15:3. See also ST 2a, 2ae, 4.1).

Between grace here and glory hereafter there is no
radical difference. They can be marked off from one another
as the unevolved from the evolved, as the child from the

adult. Between them there is neither generic (*gratia et gloria ad idem genus referuntur: quia gratia nihil est aliud quam quaedam inchoatio gloriae in nobis*—ST 2a, 2ae, 24.3 ad 2), nor specific (... *nec dicitur esse diversa perfectio naturae in statu viae et patriae quantum ad gratiam*...—*De ver.* 27.5 ad 6), nor even numerical difference (*gratia*... *ad gloriam pertinens non est alia numero a gratia*... *per quam nunc justificamur*—ST 1ae, 2ae, III.3 ad 2). There is only a difference of degree—not so great as between flower and fruit, but rather that lesser difference between green and ripe fruit (ST 1a, 2ae, 69.2).[7] Grace-life here is for St. Thomas simply unintelligible except in function of beatific vision. Modern theologians sometimes deplore the lack of emphasis laid by scholastic theology on a realized, terrestrial, presentist eschatology. They accuse scholasticism of being escapist because of its overstressing of a futurist, post-terrestrial, adventist aspect. This charge is certainly wide of the mark so far as St. Thomas goes. Perhaps more brilliantly than any other he kept in balanced tension the *already now* and the *not yet* of the revealed salvific message.

(*III*) *Created Grace*: Characteristic of full-blossomed scholasticism in general and of St. Thomas in particular is the emphasis on created grace. Indeed one might describe thirteenth century theology of the supernatural as a theology of habitual grace. "In common parlance," wrote St. Thomas, "the word *grace* denotes some habitual justifying gift" (*De ver.* 24.14: ... *communiter loquentes utuntur nomine gratiae pro aliquo dono habituali iustificante*).

Created grace is presented as a form mediating between God and man, coming from God, guaranteeing his presence

7. Also R. Morency, S.J., *L'union de grâce selon S. Thomas*, Montréal (1950), pp. 226-227.

in man, essentially and immediately ordered to God. It is a quality, habit, accident lodged in the soul (not in its faculties). In conferring grace God is acting in a different capacity from when he creates. Against the indecisiveness of early scholasticism, high scholasticism scintillates with clear-cut distinctions. Created grace affects the substance of the soul and is adequately distinct from the infused virtues lodged either in intellect (faith) or will (hope and charity). Likewise created grace as an abiding gift is neatly marked off from actual grace—an internal transient illumination of the mind or inspiration of the will preceding the infusion of sanctifying grace (e.g., *oportet praesupponi aliquod auxilium gratuitum Dei interius animam moventis, sive inspirantis bonum propositum.* This is *not* a *donum habituale*—ST 1a, 2ae, 109.6).

St. Augustine had been interested above all in the psychology of the supernatural, the process and *fieri* of justification. The early scholastics were also interested in this aspect but above all they were concerned with healing grace. St. Thomas concentrates primarily on the achieved state of justification, on describing its metaphysics. This meant concretely the study of habitual grace. St. Thomas' isolating, categorizing and underlining of created grace gave enormous force, lucidity and articulation to his theology. It is interesting to compare and contrast him with his immediate predecessors or contemporaries. Thus, like the early scholastics preceding him, William of Auxerre (c. 1150-1231) drew no distinction between grace and virtues. His theology of the supernatural is comparatively crippled and confused.[8] On the other hand, Philip the Chancellor, who greatly contributed to winning recognition for this distinction, very much advanced the

8. See J. Auer, "Der Begriff *des Ubernatürlichen," Die Entwicklung der Gnadenlehre in der Hochscholastik,* zweiter Teil, Freiburg (1951), p. 230.

theology of the supernatural. In practice this advance co-
incided with the definitive acknowledgment and painstaking
application of the aristotelic thought-patterns. It was through
this effort, which was completed and crowned by St. Thomas,
that *created grace,* defined and codified, became the pivotal
point of high scholastic theology of the supernatural.

St. Bonaventure

St. Bonaventure, who died in the same year as St. Thomas
(1274), has his own particular brand of theology of the
supernatural. Like St. Thomas, he teaches the existence of
created grace; but, unlike St. Thomas, he is not a convinced
Aristotelian and so perhaps he takes us no further than Peter
Lombard, St. Bernard and other early scholastics who also
taught that grace is an accidental form. With Bonaventure,
pastoral rather than metaphysical considerations carry weight.
He is eager to admit created grace because such an admission
better underscores man's indigence and God's munificence; it
is more religious and humble, safer and more widely removed from Pelagianism (... *pietati et humilitati magis* ...
consona ... *securior et magis recedit ab errore Pelagii*—Sent.
II, Dist. 26, a.1, q.2c).

St. Bonaventure inherits the mysticism and personalism
of St. Bernard. He effects the neoplatonic imagery of light.
Just as it is from its source, the sun, that light derives its
being and shoots forth its transforming rays, so it is from
God that grace has its worth and force. Thus grace is not
a static quality, but a flowing, dynamic, continuous becoming; it is a God-given gift, a medium flowing into man from
outside. And just as light cannot exist without the presence
of the sun, so grace involves the descent of God (*condescensio*)
which has for its counterpart the lifting up of men (*exaltatio*).
The acid-test of the possession of grace is the selflessness of

our love. Grace frees man's heart from the constriction of meanness and self-seeking and raises it to the love of God for his own sake and of one's neighbor for the love of God.

Bonaventure's theology of the supernatural is cast in the language of metaphor, not in the abstract, scientific terminology of St. Thomas. In the course of time it was Thomas' more technical theology that prevailed. The Franciscan followers of Bonaventure preserved something of his personalist approach, but, in the long run, they succumbed to the powerful Aristotelic-Thomist pressure.[9]

Why CREATED grace?

Why does high scholasticism so heavily underscore the gift of *created* grace? One reason certainly is historical: early scholasticism, despite its frequent failure to isolate habitual grace from infused virtue, was a theology of created gifts. High scholasticism took over this tendency. Then the acceptance of aristotelic metaphysics with its paraphernalia of substances, accidents, qualities, habits and virtues accelerated and favored the multiplication of distinctions as well as the emphasis on created realities. Perhaps the weightiest reason why these philosophical theologians of the heyday of scholasticism concentrated on created grace was the *realism* of their faith as Christians, thinkers and pastors of souls (for it would be a caricature to describe St. Thomas or St. Bonaventure as armchair theologians). For them the Holy Spirit was *really* present in the deified man, who was *really* loved by God. The Christian had passed from a *real* state of sin to a *real* state of justice before God; God had *really* united himself to man, *really* communicated himself. Created grace guaranteed all these realities; it was the signature of godhead in man, the

9. See Auer, *op. cit.*, pp. 232-242.

anchorage of the supernatural. Perhaps this reason of *realism* is not expressed in so many words but we can discern it clearly enough if we look hard. Thus, St. Thomas draws attention to the difference between human and divine love. Man loves what he already sees as lovable. God creates lovableness. Therefore if God really loves me anew and supernaturally, he must re-fashion me in some way, put something new into me, cause some created effect (ST 1a, 2ae, 110.1: *Pater igitur quod quamlibet Dei dilectionem sequitur aliquod bonum in creatura causatum quandoque ...*). Or again: justification means a real passage from injustice to justice through forgiveness of sins which is an act of divine love and therefore involves the infusion of created grace (ST 1a, 2ae, 113.1: *transmutatio, qua aliquis transmutatur a statu iniustitiae ad statum iustitiae per remissionem peccati ... ibid., 2: remissio = pax quae consistit in dilectione qua Deus diligit nos ... effectus ... divinae dilectionis in nobis ... est gratia*). In his *Contra gentiles* St. Thomas enunciates a metaphysical principle of universal range and validity, which in fact he uses to demonstrate the necessity of the *lumen gloriae* in the beatific vision, but which equally demonstrates the necessity of created grace in the union of deification. The principle runs:

Si aliqua duo prius fuerint non unita et postmodum uniantur, oportet quod hoc fiat per mutationem utriusque vel alterius tantum (*C. gent.* 3. 53).

If two things, previously not united, are later united, this can come about only through a change in both of them or at least in one.

If, therefore, man and God enter into a real union of love and friendship somewhere something has changed—some new reality has been brought to birth. As God cannot change, we must locate the new reality in man. We identify it with created grace, the warrant of the reality of the new union.

St. Bonaventure advances a somewhat different argument in favor of created grace:

"Cum Spiritus sanctus dicitur substantia donorum, non excluditur donum creatum, immo includitur. Non enim ob aliud dicitur nobis dari Spiritus sanctus nisi ex eo, quod sic est in nobis a Deo, ut habeatur a nobis. Tunc autem habetur a nobis, quando habitum habemus, quo possimus eo frui; et hoc est donum gratiae creatum. (Sent. 11, Dist. 26, art. 1, qu 11 ad 1)

When the Holy Spirit is referred to as the core of the gifts, the created gift is not excluded, rather it is included. Indeed for no other reason is the Holy Spirit said to be given to us except for this that he is in us from God in such a way that we possess him. But we possess him when we have a habit whereby we can enjoy him. This habit is the created gift of grace.

St. Bonaventure's thought can be epitomized in a pithy, unambiguous maxim: *habere est haberi.* To possess a *habitus* is to be possessed by God. He considers that a change is wrought in man by the very self-giving of God. The new disposition in man or created grace or the *habitus* is the upshot of the indwelling Spirit, the after-glow of the steady radiance of divine light. The soul possesses the Spirit and is possessed by him. *Habere est haberi.*

Despite allegations later made by the Reformers and modern theologians like Karl Barth, created grace for St. Thomas and St. Bonaventure is certainly not an autonomous possession of man, freeing him from God's continual saving intervention and enabling him to manipulate God and to relativize his sovereignty. On the contrary, Bonaventure and Thomas both affirm created grace in order to underscore man's

radical powerlessness before God and to exclude any righteousness flowing from purely human endeavor.

> Whereas later, scholasticism and the notion of created
> grace were attacked in order that Pelagianism might be
> the more surely avoided, the fact is that the historical
> development of the idea came about primarily as the
> result of an effort to avoid Pelagianism: St. Bonaventure
> and St. Thomas both say that if there were no created
> grace, one might think that man by his own works gives
> himself grace. Created grace, therefore, manifests the *in-
> digentia hominis;* that is why a man must be given a dis-
> position to receive justification (See St. Bonaventure, *Com-
> mentarius super Sententias* II, dist. 26, art. unicus, q. 2,
> conclusio. Ed. Quaracchi II, 635b. Quotation from C.
> Moeller and G. Philips, *The Theology of Grace,* London,
> 1961, p. 17).

> One might therefore describe created grace as being (in
> the eyes of these thinkers of the heyday of scholasticism)
> nothing less than the will of God expressing itself cease-
> lessly within the complex being of man or as an active tension
> set at work by God within man or as a permanent dynamism
> built into man's structure and lodging there an abiding and
> impelling disposition which has reality only through the
> energizing indwelling of the Spirit (*ibid.,* pp. 20-21).

(IV) Participation — Sharing the divine Nature: While St.
Thomas derived his metaphysics from Aristotle, in his religious
thinking he preserved augustinian and neoplatonic concepts
transmitted to him by his master, St. Albert the Great. He
skillfully integrated these diverse elements into his theology
of the supernatural.

Aristotle saw reality in gradations. In his analogy of being he mounted from the lesser to the greater, from the alterable to the Unmoved Mover. Thomas accepts this analogy of being but carries it to a point beyond the reach of a pagan, crowning it with the neoplatonic concept of participation as this is enriched by Augustine. He thus felicitously harmonizes analogy of being and analogy of faith.[10] He is quite aware of his indebtedness. Thus having stated that charity in us is *quaedam participatio divinae caritatis* he adds:

Hic enim modus loquendi consuetus est apud Platonicos; quorum doctrinis imbutus fuit Augustinus (ST 2a, 2ae, 23.2 ad 1).	This way of speaking was familiar to the "Platonics" whose teaching inspired Augustine.

Participation is a key concept in St. Thomas' theology of the supernatural. By the time he came to write his *Quaestiones disputatae de veritate* (1256-1259) he had become deeply struck by 2 P 1.4: the Father through Christ makes us sharers in the divine nature. *Divinae naturae consortes*—a lapidary phrase beloved by Fathers of the Church, theologians and the shapers of the Liturgy. It became for St. Thomas the epitome of the supernatural. He identified grace with a sharing in the divine nature or goodness (*ipsa participatio divinae bonitatis quae est gratia* . . .–ST 1a, 2ae, 110.2 ad 2; see *ibid.*, 3; *gratia nihil est aliud quam quaedam participata similitudo divinae naturae secundum illud*, 2 P 1.4–ST 3a, 62.1). Likewise, the virtue of charity is *participatio quaedam Spiritus sancti* (ST 2a, 2ae, 23.3 ad 3; cf. *ibid.*, 24.2: charity is in us *per infusionem Spiritus sancti* . . . *cuius participatio in nobis est ipsa caritas creata*). Supernatural bliss (*beatitudo naturam hominis excedens*) is presented in the same way: it is a goal

10. *Ibid.*, pp. 237-238.

which man can attain only by divine might, according to a certain sharing in godhead as one reads in St. Peter (*ad quam* [*beatitudinem*] *homo sola divina virtute pervenire potest, secundum quandam divinitatis participationem secundum quod dicitur* 2 P 1.4 *quod per Christum facti sumus consortes divinae naturae*—ST 1a, 2ae, 62.1).

Participation, of course, is a philosophical as well as a theological concept; it is accessible to reason as well as to faith; it is found in both the natural and the supernatural order. Life, knowledge, love, beauty, as found in creatures, are analogical participations of these attributes as they exist in God. Through participation in the created order there occurs no formal divine self-communication. But this is precisely what supernatural participation involves, which, consequently, is for St. Thomas the highest possible participation affecting created reality. Through it, the godhead, which belongs to God in an essential way, is communicated to the creature in an accidental way. In so far as it implies a formal sharing in the godhead itself,[11] supernatural participation must be singled out from all other sorts. For St. Thomas it is a constitutent expression of the supernatural.

St. Thomas defines supernatural participation as (I) requiring a created gift which (II) cannot be substantial but only accidental.

As to (I)—wherever there is supernatural participation, there must be some created gift whether this be sanctifying grace or infused virtue or *lumen gloriae*. Thus, for example, having asserted that man's beatitude is through participation, St.

11. "Una partecipazione formale della stessa Deità in sè" — C. Fabro, *La nozione metafisica di partecipazione secondo S. Tommaso d'Aquino*, 2nd ed. Turin (1950), p. 304; see also S. I. Dockx, O.P., *Fils de Dieu par grâce*, (1948), pp. 31-32.

Thomas immediately adds that this sharing in divine blessedness is something created: *ipsa autem participatio beatitudinis, secundum quam homo dicitur beatus, aliquid creatum est* (ST 1a, 2ae, 3.1 ad 1).

As to (II)—his own plain words need no comment:

Et quia gratia est supra naturam humanam, non potest esse quod sit substantia aut forma substantialis; sed est forma accidentalis ipsius animae. Id enim quod substantialiter est in Deo, accidentaliter fit in anima participante divinam bonitatem . . . (ST 1a, 2ae, 110.2 ad 2).	And because grace transcends human nature it can not be a substance or a substantial form; but it is an accidental form of the soul itself. For what is substantially in God, accidentally affects the soul that shares in the divine goodness.

Restriction?

Sometimes St. Thomas writes about this supernatural participation unrestrictedly (e.g., *lumen gratiae, quod est participatio divinae naturae*—ST 1a, 2ae, 110.3; *ipsa participatio divinae bonitatis quae est gratia*—ibid., 2 ad 2). At other times he employs attenuating phrases: *quodammodos, quaedams* and *similitudos* (QUODAMMODO *fit homo particeps divinae naturae*—ST 1a, 2ae, 62.1 ad 1; *donum gratiae . . . nihil aliud sit quam* QUAEDAM *participatio divinae naturae*—ibid., 112.1; *homo . . . participat secundum* QUAMDAM SIMILITUDINEM *naturam divinam per* QUAMDAM *regenerationem . . .* ibid., 110.4; *. . . gratia nihil est aliud, quam* QUAEDAM *participata* SIMILITUDO *divinae naturae . . .* —ST 3a, 62.1).

Various explanations of St. Thomas' reserves are forthcoming. Cornelio Fabro (who refers to the *similitudo* as *una "degradazione"*) thinks that St. Thomas is drawing a firm line of demarcation between a Christian's sharing in the divine nature on the one hand and, on the other, the plenitude with which the godhead possesses itself or communicates itself to Christ at the incarnation (*pienezza con cui la Divinità possiede se stessa, o si è communicata al Cristo—op. cit.,* p. 305). He quotes St. Thomas:

Gratia quae est accidens est quaedam similitudo divinitatis, participata in homine. Per incarnationem autem humana natura non dicitur participasse similitudinem aliquam divinae naturae: sed dicitur esse coniuncta ipsi divinae naturae in persona Filii (ST 3a, 2.10 ad 1; cf. *Comp. theol.* 215).	Grace, which is an accident, is a certain likeness of godhead shared in by man. But by the taking of flesh human nature is not said to have shared in some likeness to the divine nature. Rather it is said to be joined to the divine nature itself in the person of the Son.

Rondet suggests that St. Thomas identifies unrestricted participation not with the grace-life on earth but with that of the beatific vision (*. . . ad plenam participationem divinitatis quae vera est hominis beatitudo . . .*—ST 3a, 1.2—see *Gratia Christi,* 1948, p. 199).

Probably we should combine all three explanations (God's self-possession, his self-communication to Christ, the consummation of the beatific vision) or, better, use now one, now another according to the subject-matter under discussion. What, however, must not be lost sight of is the content which St. Thomas assigns to *all* supernatural participation, even the most lowly. This content can be expressed as self-communication of God himself implying our deification, our re-birth, the indwelling Spirit, adoptive sonship. St. Thomas' laconicism, the impassivity and abstraction of his formal, technical language must not be allowed to gloss this over.

Participation and divinization

As to deification, from the very fact that St. Thomas' habit is to use words so sparingly and circumspectly, his statements are all the more impressive. "God," he writes, "is felicity through his own being. But men have felicity through participation just as through participation they are called gods" (... *sicut et dii per participationem dicuntur*—ST 1a, 2ae, 3.1 ad 1). The same idea figures in a passage quoted in the Office of Corpus Christi:[12]

Unigenitus . . . Dei Filius, suae divinitatis volens nos esse participes, naturam nostram assumpsit, ut homines deos faceret factus homo.	The only-begotten Son of God, wanting to make us sharers in his godhead, took up our nature so that by becoming man he might make men gods.

St. Thomas' notion of sharing in the divine nature, despite its stiff scholastic dress, is fundamentally the same as

12. M. Grabmann lists the *Officium de festo Corporis Christi ad mandatum Urbani Papae IV* amongst St. Thomas' genuine works. In particular, about the lessons (from which our quotation is taken) he asserts: "Dass die Lektionen zur zweiten Nokturn von Thomas stammen, unterliegt keinem Zweifel" *Die echten Schriften des Hl. Thomas von Aquin*, Münster (1920), p. 233. We should also note ST 1a, 12.5 where, dealing with the *lumen gloriae* in the beatific vision, St. Thomas writes: *secundum hoc lumen efficiuntur deiformes, i.e., Deo similes.*

the Greek patristic theme of man's divinization. This is evinced
by the following passage which gathers together much of
St. Thomas' thinking on the supernatural while at the same
time being strangely reminiscent of the style of argument
used by Cyril of Alexandria for the godhead of the Holy
Spirit:

*Donum autem gratiae excedit
omnem facultatem naturae
creatae, cum nihil aliud sit
quam quaedam participatio
divinae naturae, quae excedit
omnem aliam naturam. Et
ideo impossibile est quod aliqua creatura gratiam causet.
Sic enim necesse est quod solus Deus deificet, communi-
cando consortium divinae naturae per quamdam similitu-
dinis participationem, sicut
impossibile est quod aliquid
igniat nisi solus ignis* (ST 1a,
2ae, 112.1).

But the gift of grace is beyond every capacity of created nature, since it is nothing
else than a certain sharing in
the divine nature which is
superior to every other nature.
Therefore it is impossible for
any creature to cause grace.
For so it must be God alone
who deifies, by communicating a sharing in the divine
nature through a certain participation of likeness—just as
it is impossible for anything
except fire to cause fire.

In this passage one observes the attenuating phrases remarked
on above. Above all one notes how St. Thomas couples together divinization and participation—both of which mean
God's self-communication.

That the personal presence of God is granted through
supernatural participation is illustrated in *Summa Theologica*
where St. Thomas is dealing with the Holy Spirit (ST 1a,
38.1). He has broached the question how one can *have* a
person, particularly a divine Person. He replies: we are said

to *have* what we can use and enjoy at will. In this sense a divine Person can be *had* only by a rational creature and one united to God. Infrarational creatures can, of course, be governed by a divine Person but not to the point of their being able to enjoy a divine Person, drawing on the riches of his personality. By contrast, a rational creature may on occasions reach this privileged position—if, for example, he can, according to his own fancy, know God truly and love him soundly because he has become a sharer in the divine Word and the Love proceeding from him (*... cum ... fit particeps divini Verbi et procedentis amoris ...*). However, such possession of a divine Person, the exclusive dignity of the rational creature, does not arise from human resources. It must be given from on high (*oportet quod hoc ei desuper datur*).

Despite the dryness and impersonality of his style, St. Thomas plainly conceives participation as personal encounter between God and man, as re-birth and re-creation (*homo ... participat ... naturam divinam per quamdam regenerationem, sive recreationem*—ST 1a, 2ae, 110.4), love and friendship (ST 2a, 2ae, 23.1; *In Ioan.* 13.7; 15.3), adoptive sonship (*dignitatem gratiae, per quam homo consors factus divinae naturae, adoptatur in filium Dei, cui debetur haereditas ex ipso iure adoptionis ...* —ST 1a, 2ae, 114.3. In his commentary on *Romans*, St. Thomas makes clear that our inheritance as sons is God himself: *Bonum ... principale quo Deus dives est, est ipsemet ... ipsum Deum adipiscuntur filii Dei pro haereditate*—*In Rom.* 8:3 Marietti (1953) (par. 647) and the indwelling Spirit:

Spiritus autem sanctus, quum Deus sit, per suam substantiam mentem inhabitat et sui participatione bonos facit (C.

But the Holy Spirit, since he is God, dwells substantially in the minds of men and by a sharing in himself, makes

gent. 4.18. See *De carit.* 1;   them good.
In Ioann. 14.6; 15.5; ST 1a,
43. 3, 5, 6).

"Sharing in the divine nature"—this means for St. Thomas being taken aside and lifted above the world, union with God, true knowledge, friendship (*electi . . . elevati supra mundum . . . effecti participes divinitatis et coniuncti Deo . . . vera Dei notitia scilicet per veram fidem et devotum amorem . . . amici Dei . . . —In Ioann.* 15.4 Marietti par. 2043). "Sharing in the divine nature"—this is assuredly one of St. Thomas' favorite phrases (of it Auer asserts: "ungewöhnlich häufig gebraucht" —*op. cit.*, p. 238). However nowhere does he embroider it theologically with the speculations of subsequent Thomists. This fact has prompted Auer to suggest that for St. Thomas this phrase was a treasure for contemplation rather than a theme for speculation. "Sharing in the divine nature" is therefore more than an epitome of St. Thomas' theology of the supernatural; it is also a threshold to his mysticism. It reveals not only the depth and acumen of the prince of scholastic theologians but also the yearnings of the saint.

Chapter 4

In the history of theology, nominalism is an important episode with far-reaching effects. Today in the re-assessment of reformation-positions and in the ecumenical dialogue, the term keeps cropping up. It may, therefore, be profitable to glance backwards once more to its theology of the supernatural—especially since a recent work (*The Harvest of Medieval Theology—Gabriel Biel and Late Medieval Nominalism* by Heiko A. Oberman, Harvard, 1963), despite its impressive scholarship, engenders certain misgivings.

Nominalism was a reaction against the Aristotelianism of high (thirteenth century) scholasticism; in particular against the proud, inter-locking synthesis of St. Thomas. It was furthermore, a nostalgia for early (1050-1220) scholasticism, which, for the nominalist, represented "the golden age of a united theological vision and vocabulary, abruptly broken off by the Babylonian disintegration of theological language caused by the philosophical bias of Thomists and Scotists"

(Oberman, *op. cit.,* p. 148). Nominalism is the *via moderna* standing opposed to the *via antiqua* of thomism and scotism. In the ensuing struggle between the two ways, the universities of Europe—Paris, Oxford, Heidelberg, Tübingen, Vienna, Erfurt, Leipzig—succumbed, one after another, to the advances of nominalism. Cologne held out as the bastion of thomism. By the time of Luther, nominalism enjoyed a respectability rivalling that of the *via antiqua.* Theologians of the counter-reformation such as John Eck and James Lainez and many bishops at Trent had either undergone its influence or at least held it in esteem.[1]

Scotus

The seeds of nominalism were sown by Duns Scotus (1266-1308) who bridges high with late (fourteenth and fifteenth centuries) scholasticism or nominalism. For Scotus, justification is no longer the single, simple, instantaneous event with multiple facets that it was for St. Thomas (ST 1a, 2ae, 113.7 and 8). Scotus breaks it up into its components, and drives a wedge between the infusion of grace and the remission of sins, between created and uncreated grace. On the other hand, he surrenders the hard-won, clear-cut distinction between the infused virtue of charity lodged in the will and sanctifying grace lodged in the substance of the soul. Following the inclination of St. Bonaventure, Scotus locates both in the will and proclaims a formal, not a real distinction between them. He lays great stress on the sovereign freedom

1. Oberman, *The Harvest of Medieval Theology — Gabriel Biel and Late Medieval Nominalism,* pp. 17-21; 426-427. Piet Fransen holds that the whole doctrine of sacramental efficacy as inherited until recently is "stamped with the trademark of fourteenth century nominalism," *Christian Revelation and World Religions,* London (1967), pp. 70-74.

of God's will and offers this, rather than innate characteristics
and ontological endowments, as the explanation of all things:
of the opposition between good and bad; as to why this is
good and that is bad; as to why a meritorious action wins
an eternal reward; as to why remission of sin and infusion
of grace are bound together. Scotus holds that God might,
absolutely speaking, infuse grace into a man persisting in
serious sin.[2] In short, the main tenets of nominalism appear
already in Scotus: the accent on God's freedom; the distinction
between God's ordained and his absolute power; the possibility
of the co-existence of grace and sin; a tendency to explain
the supernatural not so much by created grace as by God's
acception.[3]

The positions adumbrated by Scotus were taken up and
systematically developed by the nominalists.[4] The nominalists
were represented in France by Durandus of Saint-Pourçain
(ob. 1334), Pierre d'Ailly (ob. 1420) and Gerson (ob. 1429);
in Italy by Gregory of Rimini (ob. 1358); in Germany by
Gabriel Biel. An Englishman, William of Ockham, was the
chief architect of the impressively coherent structure of
nominalism.

2. About *gratia* and *culpa* Scotus writes: *Deus potest de potentia
sua facere unum et non creare aliud, et ita expellere culpam etsi non
infundat gratiam et e converso.* Reportata Parisiensia Lib. 4, dist. 16,
quaest. 2, schol. 1 n. 5.

3. J. Auer charges Scotus with dismantling the structure of the
supernatural: "... fast vollständig zerbricht die Struktur des Übernatürlichen bei Scotus dadurch vor allem, dass an Stelle der Leistungen der
Gnade die letzte Wirkung der Gnade, die göttliche Akzeptation allein
gesetzt wird...," *Die Entwicklung der Gnadenlehre in der Hochscholastik*, Freiburg (1951), 2, p. 254.

4. E. Amann writes: "en un point capital, la théorie de la justification,
le nominalisme ne contredit pas Duns Scot, mais le continue; et sur
ce problème, on a pu classer Scot dans 'l'École nominaliste,'" DTC
11, 878.

Ockham

Ockham was born in a village of that name in Surrey, probably about 1285. He became a Franciscan, studied theology at Oxford and acquired the status of *Inceptor* (i.e., he had completed the cycle of studies required for a Master's degree). Ockham never gained the more distinguished title of *Magister regens* probably because his career was cut short owing to the reaction provoked by the ideas he was disseminating. He is known to history as the *Venerabilis Inceptor*. Quitting Oxford about 1319, he spent four years at Avignon. In 1326 a select papal commission judged 51 propositions, drawn from his writings, deserving of censure. In fact Ockham's theology was never condemned. He did, however, together with his General, Michael of Cesena, fall foul of Pope John XXII over the interpretation of Franciscan poverty and was excommunicated in 1328. Escaping from Avignon Ockham went first to Pisa then to Munich where he joined forces with Louis of Bavaria, the Pope's archenemy. For about 20 years Ockham figured as a stormy controversialist. He died at Munich, according to some in 1347 (G. Gál, *New Cath. Enc.*, 14, 932), according to others in 1349.[5]

Though Ockham derives some of his central positions from Scotus, he does not hesitate to attack and refute him.[6] He also censures Aristotle, particularly for confusing the regular with the necessary.[7] For Ockham, abstract knowledge has nothing to do with existence; at best it is a logic of possibilities indirectly referable to reality. He sees the world

5. R. Guelluy, *Philosophie et théologie chez Guillaume d'Ockham*, Louvain (1947), p. 13. Guelluy remarks: "Ockham est aussi célèbre que mal connu ... On ne connait ni la date de sa naissance, ni celle de sa mort," *ibid.*, 1.

6. *Ibid.*, pp. 67-76; 143-146.

7. *Ibid.*, p. 364.

as contingent and as composed of individuals lacking all necessary interconnection. The only adequate ground for asserting any casual relationship between two phenomena is empirical: the observation of regular sequence. Causality is not, therefore, an insight grounded on the actual relationship between things; it is simply a way of reflecting on experience. In fact man can have no sure knowledge of anything beyond the intuition of an immediately present sense object. Hence arguments depending on man's experience of the *de facto* order have the value only of probabilities. There is no room for any proof of God's existence based on efficient and final causality.

We are not concerned with Ockham as a formal logician and philosopher, (as such his renown is by no means dimmed in the twentieth century). We are interested in the theologian. His philosophic speculations always remain intimately linked with his theological view of the free, almighty, evermerciful God. A characteristic feature of his theology is the distinction between God's ordinary and his absolute power, by means of which Ockham emphasized that the present order of nature and the supernatural is not necessary but freely established by a God who might just as easily have constructed any other arrangement not self-contradictory. As Ockham's theology of the supernatural is less fully developed than that of his true disciple Biel, we can discuss it when we deal with Biel below. For the moment we remark that it is incontestable that Ockham, with his critical attitude and vigorous opinions, contributed to the breaking up of the high scholastic synthesis. At the same time it must be recognized that his accentuating of particulars against universals, of intuition against abstraction, of induction against deduction opened the door to advances in science. Gál makes an interesting observation: Ockham, he writes, "usually receives a fairer treatment from those who have studied his writings thoroughly ... than from authors of scholastic handbooks" (*op. cit.*, 934). P. Vignaux is an outstanding example of those who know Ockham thoroughly and treat him fairly ("Nominalisme" DTC 11, pp. 717-784).

Biel

Gabriel Biel was born at Speyer in the first quarter of the fifteenth century. About 1432 he was ordained priest, studied arts at Heidelberg where he took his master's degree in 1438. Later he applied himself to theology at the universities, first of Erfurt (where the *via moderna* held sway) and then of Cologne (where thomism was still the vogue). From a letter of Pope Sixtus V written in December 1474 we gather that Biel became *Licentiatus in theologia*. Biel was not one-eyed. He knew well and he often quoted both St. Thomas and Duns Scotus. However he hailed as one of the signs of progress in his day the fact that Thomas, though a canonized saint, was openly contradicted in the universities. Ockham, rather than anyone else, was the master whom Biel most admired. He rated him as the deepest seeker for truth and he clung to his teaching (... *profundissimus veritatis indagator Guilhelmus Occam cuius doctrinam tamquam clariorem frequentius imitor* ... —quoted by Oberman, *op. cit.*, p. 54 note 77).

Biel's middle age was devoted to three main pursuits: preaching at the cathedral of Mainz; supporting Adolph von Nassau against Diether von Isenburg as claimant to the archiepiscopal see of Mainz; associating with the Brethren of the Common Life. In 1484 he was appointed to the theological faculty of the recently founded university of Tübingen. His influence led to the university's adopting the *via moderna*. In 1485 and 1489 Biel held office as Rector of the university. After his second term, when already, probably, in his seventies, he retired from active academic life and spent his last years in the new Brethren House at Einsiedel in Schönbuch where he died on Dec. 7, 1495. His life was marked by a deep concern for the Church; he was zealous in furthering the welfare of souls (his own and others); he faced with tenacity and dedication the rigors of exacting scholarship.

Characteristics of nominalist theology of the supernatural

Although (as we have seen) Biel is not the chief architect of nominalism, he is nevertheless its leading spokesman—at least for the theology of the supernatural. Hence it is to his writings that we shall pay attention.

A pre-eminent characteristic of nominalist theology is its distinction between God's *absolute* and his *ordained* power.

These two phrases (*de potentia absoluta* and *de potentia ordinata*) were not an invention of the nominalists. They can be traced back to the dawn of scholasticism. But prior to nominalism their position was peripheral. Duns Scotus drew them closer to the center of theology. Under the nominalists they became master-keys to unlock theological speculations and release the inhibitions resulting from a dogmatic system.

This distinction of two powers does not in itself (nor did it for the nominalists) imply two really distinct capacities in God, who is ineffable simplicity and who directs his influence to the world outside him with undivided omnipotence. This distinction is a necessary fabrication imposed on God by the human mind in its search to explain the *real* as contrasted with other *possible* worlds. It does not imply that God oscillates between an ordinate and absolute behavior; nor that he acts now with, and later without reason. It does, on the contrary, mean that God can do everything that does not involve a contradiction, whether or not he has actually decreed to do so. There are many things that God can do which in fact he does not choose to do—this is the concept of his absolute power.

The *absolute power* of God is, therefore, subject only to the law of his own being or (which is the same thing) the law of non-contradiction. It leaves out of count the actually existing order. Thus, according to his absolute power, God might declare a man guiltless without giving him grace, or he might infuse grace into a man persisting in grave sinfulness; or he might grant the beatific vision without inherent grace. This, at any rate, is how the nominalists conceived God's absolute power.

The *ordinary* or *directed* power of God covers the arrangement of the universe as established by God or his way of acting towards the created and contingent world in fact existing "outside" him. *Potentia ordinata,* then, is God's power as regulated and directed according to the natural and revealed laws which he himself has framed. It affirms that the actual order, whether natural or supernatural, is not *necessarily* but *freely* constituted by God. This present order, therefore, has a necessity arising exclusively from the fact that God has channeled his might through and into it. In fact God could have created one or other component or co-efficient of present reality without being obliged to create its partner.

De potentia ordinata, the infusion of grace, the indwelling of the Holy Spirit and acceptance by God coincide—but without compelling necessity. This does not mean that the stable, contingent order of revelation decreed by God according to his *ordained power* is arbitrary. On the contrary it is directed by God's wisdom. However it is unpredictable. Thus in the pre-mosaic period, the mosaic stage defied human forecast. Likewise in the mosaic period, the era of the Church could not be foreseen.

To elucidate his thought, Biel cites an OT example. Before

Christianity unbaptized babies might gain entry into heaven through circumcision. The NT imposed the necessity of baptism. This proves (Biel contends) that baptism, though normally required in Christianity, has no absolute necessity. Hence he concludes: revelation is historical not metaphysical. Likewise natural laws can be suspended *de potentia absoluta*. Thus secondary causes are enabled to achieve results beyond their capacity under the régime of God's *ordained power*. Miracles are a reminder that nature is not a closed, self-contained and iron-clad system.

God's *ordinary power* is addressed to the past events in the history of salvation which have shaped the present: creation, fall, redemption. The Church inaugurates the stable and definitive salvific phase that will reach down to doomsday. Faith is concerned with God's dealing with men according to his *ordained power*.

To claim that the inherent value of acts or states can exact a heavenly reward apart from God's acceptation of them is (in Biel's eyes) to cross from the order of *ordained* to that of *absolute* power. It is, besides, to suggest that the created and the mutable can influence the uncreated and the immutable (Oberman, *op. cit.*, 169). Biel sees God's gratuitous self-giving love manifested in his choice from all eternity of the particular salvific economy in which our lives unfold.

Optimism

A second characteristic in the nominalist theology of the supernatural is its optimism, its high esteem for man's native capacities, unaided by grace, even after the fall. Sin has not barred man's path to right doing. The will still retains its freedom and can obey the dictates of conscience. Biel views the main hindrance to man's good behavior not so much in the absence of grace as of sound knowledge. The will, though able to choose the best set before it, depends on reason to pick out what it ought to will. It is not so much will as reason that is the root of all virtue. Biel envisaged the Church's primary role to be not the dispensing of grace but the furnishing of full and correct information about God. This, if personally pondered on, would (he felt sure) inevitably promote moral betterment.[8] Because of their optimism the nominalists taught that man has it in his own hands to turn his back on sin and, by striving his uttermost, to gain the love of God above everything else.

Doing one's best

Closely allied to the second, is the third feature of nominalism. It can be summed up in the maxim: "God will not withhold his grace from the man who does his best" (*facienti quod in se est, Deus non denegat gratiam*). Doing one's best meant for Biel rallying all one's natural forces, deliberately making face against one's sinfulness and resolutely turning towards God, pleading for his pardon and help. It meant ceasing to sin, casting down the barriers of sin. It meant reflecting on God and his attributes, along with the persistent endeavor, ever more successful, to love God for his own sake and beyond anything else.

Congruous merit

A fourth ingredient in the nominalist theology of the supernatural is congruous or semi merit. This term covers the situation of a man who, prior to the infusion of sanctifying grace, is busy trying his hardest to come to God and is thus eliciting many ethically good acts (these are conceived by

8. Oberman, *op. cit.*, p. 165.

Biel as the framework or under-strutting over which God lays the adornment of grace). Nominalism taught that such actions preparatory to justification (in this context, called by Biel *first grace*) are congruously meritorious i.e., they can earn from God the reward of sanctifying grace. Here are Biel's words:

Anima obicis remotione ac bono motu in deum ex arbitrii libertate elicito gratiam potest mereri de congruo. Probatur quia actum facientis quod in se est deus acceptat ad tribuendum gratiam primam, non ex debito iustitiae, sed ex sua liberalitate. Sed anima removendo obicem, cessando ab actu et consensu peccati et eliciendo bonum motum in deum tamquam in suum principium et finem, facit quod in se est. Ergo actum remotionis obicis et bonum motum in deum acceptat deus de sua liberalitate ad infundendum gratiam (II Sent. d. 27, q. 1, art. 2, concl. 4K; Oberman, 172, note 80).	By casting down barriers and by a freely elicited good movement towards God, the soul can merit congruously. The proof of this is that God accepts the act of the man doing his best in order to give him first grace, not according to a claim in justice but out of his own munificence. But the soul that removes an obstacle, that stops itself from sinning and consenting to sin, that elicits a good movement towards God its beginning and end, does its best. Hence God, out of munificence accepts the act of casting down barriers and the good movement towards God as a reason for the infusion of grace.

The man who merits congruously is not yet God's friend but he is trying his hardest to become such. Because he has not yet attained to the state of friendship, his behavior, however noble ethically, remains disproportionate to the love with which God awaits him. In no sense, then, can congruously

meritorious actions be set on a footing of equality or proportion with the gift of God's love or infused grace. Nevertheless this in fact is the reward with which God crowns
them. Because of the vast disproportion dividing deed from
reward, there can be no question of contractual justice. God's
reward flows solely from his bounty and largesse; it cannot
be claimed in virtue of any previous pact. For Biel this field
of congruous merit furnishes a privileged and pre-eminent
display of God's free initiative, of his sheer munificence, of
his overriding love and of the sovereign gratuity of the gift
of grace.

Grace — acceptation

The final and perhaps salient feature of nominalist theology of the supernatural is its complex attitude to the state
of grace, condign merit and acceptation.

The man who does his best will (as we have just seen)
receive the reward of the state of grace which, according
to Biel, he earns congruously. Biel, however, is unequivocal
and emphatic that until this "first" grace has been infused
there can be no question about condign merit. The root of
condign merit is the state of grace.

The state of grace is the state of divine friendship. It
implies the infusion of habitual or created grace which Biel
regarded as in fact necessary for salvation *de potentia ordinata*—though *de potentia absoluta* God could accept a
man to everlasting life without it. The state of grace implies,
besides, the indwelling of the Holy Spirit together with incorporation into Christ and membership of his visible Church.
It also links the converted sinner in a bond of love with Christ.

A man in such a state is able to elicit acts that stand in
some proportion to his supernatural last end. These deliberate-

ly elicited good deeds partake of the dignity of his state and are now *condignly* meritorious. That is to say, they come within the context of contractual justice. God has freely bound himself to reward such acts. He thus allows man to have a claim in justice on a divine reward. So the man in the state of grace can merit condignly increase of grace; moreover if he dies in this state, he merits condignly heaven. God *accepts* the works of such a man and pays him his well-earned wages of everlasting life.

Nominalist *acceptation* is often spoken of as uncreated grace. It presupposes a pact in strict justice. It rises from a necessity anchored in God's own being and within the context of his eternal decree (about which revelation informs us) that actions done by his loyal friends will be recompensed with everlasting life. This acceptation presupposes a *proportion* between man's work and his reward.

Biel writes:

Invenitur aliquid proportionale in actu meritorio: nam ibi est spiritus sanctus inhabitans per gratiam tamquam primum movens, qui porportionatur ultimo fini trinitati deo ... Ibi est gratia gratum faciens supernaturalis a deo infusa tamquam semen gloriae. Et sicut semen arboris virtute continet totum arborem, ita gratia virtute continet praemia. Eo modo etiam quo praemium est infinitum et gratia est infinita (II Sent., d. 27, q. 1, art. 2. concl. 1F).

In the meritorious act there is some proportion: for *there* is the Holy Spirit indwelling through grace as first mover, and he is in proportion to the last end, the triune God .... *There* is supernatural sanctifying grace infused by God as a seed of glory. And just as the seed of a tree contains the whole tree in embryo, so grace contains remuneration in embryo. And grace is infinite in the same sense in which the reward is infinite.

Biel cannot be charged with overlooking the self-communication of the three-personed God to man. According to him, the infusion of sanctifying grace is always accompanied by the inhabitation of the Holy Spirit, Christ, the Trinity.[9] Indeed nominalism's accent on acceptation is equivalent to an accent on uncreated rather than created grace.[10]

Oberman protests against equating Biel's theology with a proto-Protestant doctrine of imputed or forensic justification. There seem grounds for holding that nominalism is a critical reaction against the prominence assigned to created grace by thomism. But nominalism undoubtedly demands inherent grace and indwelling Spirit; it does not, therefore, teach God's acceptation of man by imputing to him a purely extrinsic righteousness.

Evaluation

J. Rivière warmly defends the orthodoxy of the nominalist school: "il serait contre toute justice de la (i.e., "école nominaliste") mettre en opposition avec la foi" ("Justification" DTC 8 2129).

On the other hand Oberman stigmatizes "as essentially Pelagian"[11] Biel's doctrine of justification; and "as at least semi-Pelagian"[12] that of nominalism in general.

Many of Biel's statements lend color to Oberman's charge. For example Biel's treatment of congruous merit seems to suggest that acts preparatory to justification (which he expressly denominates *first* grace) are themselves produced without any grace and yet *infallibly* call down the infusion of grace (see DTC 8 2128-2129). Here is a passage in which Biel

9. *Ibid.*, pp. 353-356.
10. *Ibid.*, p. 354.
11. *Ibid.*, p. 177.
12. *Ibid.*, p. 426.

appears to teach that a purely human appeal to God must be answered with sanctifying grace:

> God takes notice of those who seek their refuge with him. Otherwise there would be iniquity in him. (*Aliter in eo esset iniquitas*). But it is impossible that there be iniquity in him. Therefore, it is impossible that he would not receive those who take refuge with him. But if one does one's very best, one takes refuge with him. Therefore, it is necessary that God receive one. This reception, now, is the infusion of grace. (*Ergo necesse est quod ipsum recipiat. Recipit autem infundendo gratiam.* II Sent. d. 27, q. 1, art. 2, concl. 4K; Oberman, 174-175).

Biel's statement here seems to amount to this: exclusively human prayer can exact from God not merely ordinary providential help or simply *gratia sanans* but even *gratia elevans*, internal, entitatively supernatural grace. If indeed this accurately expresses his thought then he is (as Oberman asserts) certainly semi-pelagian (see Denz. 373).

Nominalism not semi-pelagianism

However there are reasons that make one hesitate to go along with Oberman's verdict. First, Oberman himself, despite his plain, academic prowess, does not seem quite free from tendentiousness. He strongly and repeatedly protests against classifying nominalism as a decadence of medieval theology. "... The often-asserted thesis of the 'disintegration of late medieval thought' proves to be untenable. It is precisely to call attention to this fact that we have chosen as our title *The Harvest of Medieval Theology*." [13] To put it simply and

13. *Ibid.*, p. 423.

bluntly—Oberman's position seems reducible to this syllogism and its sequel:

> Nominalism is an authentic and respectable medieval representative of "what has come to be known as Roman Catholicism." [14]
> But nominalism is at least semi-pelagian.
> Therefore what has come to be known as Roman Catholicism is semi-pelagian. Hence the lutheran accusation that the Church had abandoned her pristine anti-pelagian orthodoxy was well-founded—as was, likewise, the protestant revolt against Roman Catholicism.

Secondly, we need to distinguish in nominalism the *content* of its theology of the supernatural from the *language* in which this is cast. Reading Biel in the light of post-tridentine theology can do him great disservice. Undoubtedly, for the modern reader, there lurks an ambiguity in his language. This would seem to be at least one reason why nominalism became antiquated through the council of Trent. One may legitimately wonder whether Biel, in his discussions about man's preparation for justification and his capacity for congruous merit, asserts anything beyond what later scholastic theologians would more clearly articulate under the technical concept of *negative* disposition for grace. Assuredly Biel's heavy underscoring of the initiative, generosity and gratuity of God's response to the man who is congruously meriting seems to endorse such an interpretation. Oberman himself fairly insists that much of Biel's theology is pastoral and that to understand him faithfully we must take into consideration not only his academic writings but also his sermons. About one of these, where Biel urges that the selfless love of God displayed

14. *Ibid.*, p. 428.

SUPERNATURAL IN LATE SCHOLASTICISM

in the passion can move the sinner to dispose himself for
the coming of the Holy Spirit, Oberman comments: "At this
point Biel preaches a stern anti-pelagian doctrine of unmerited love."[15] It may be queried whether the nominalists,
despite deficiencies in language and system, ever lost this
vision of unmerited love and ever fell into pelagianism. That
they did not, would seem to emerge from the respectability
they enjoyed in catholic circles up to Trent, and also from
the fact that they were never censured.[16] Perhaps the problem
of nominalist orthodoxy is no more serious than that of the
council of Trent or of the Fathers or indeed of Scripture
itself: i.e., the problem of the tension between the overriding primary causality of God and the utterly derived and
secondary causality of man in the field of the supernatural
and in the affair of his salvation.[17]

Defective theology of the supernatural

However nominalism, even if its orthodoxy is beyond re-
proach, is far from furnishing a satisfactory theology of the
supernatural. Ambiguity of language might be one reason
why it became obsolete after Trent. A larger and weightier
reason is its inherent defects as a theology of the supernatural. We single out just two of its tenets: (1) *de potentia*

15. *Ibid.*, p. 349.
16. Two "theologians of nominalistic leanings, Nicolaus of Autre-
court and John of Mirecourt were indeed forced to recant (1347); but
the relation of the theses condemned to the main body of Ockham's
thought was not regarded by the late medieval nominalistic schoolmen
as of such intimacy as to affect the status and orthodoxy of the *Venerabilis Inceptor*. Nominalism remained a valid option in the rapidly
growing number of universities." Oberman, *op. cit.*, p. 426.
17. On the anti-pelagianism of Ockham, note Vignaux, *art. cit.*,
DTC 8, pp. 774-776.

absoluta God could give the beatific vision to a man lacking inherent grace; (11) *de potentia absoluta* God might infuse habitual grace into a man clinging to serious sin. These affirmations seem to involve an abuse of the distinction between God's *potentia absoluta* and his *potentia ordinata* because they imply a defective understanding of the entitatively supernatural.

St. Thomas has left us an excellent and sobering statement on the understanding of God's omnipotence:

In nobis, in quibus potentia et essentia aliud est a voluntate et intellectu, et iterum intellectus aliud a sapientia, et voluntas aliud a iustitia, potest esse aliquid in potentia quod non potest esse in voluntate iusta, vel in intellectu sapiente. Sed in Deo est idem potentia et essentia et iustitia. Unde nihil potest esse in potentia divina quod non possit esse in voluntate iusta ipsius et intellectu sapiente eius (ST 1a, 25. 5 ad 1).	In us whose capacity and essence are different from will and intellect, and again whose intellect is different from wisdom and will from justice, there can be something in our capacity which is not in our just will or in our wise intellect. But in God capacity and essence and justice are the same thing. Hence nothing can be in divine capacity which is not in God's just will and in his wise intellect.

The nominalist upholding of these two tenets involves, on the basis of an adequate appreciation of the entitatively supernatural, a metaphysical contradiction which consequently cannot be justified by invoking the distinction of God's twin power.

To take the first. This tenet means that in *patria* man can be united with the first Person of the Trinity as his adoptive

Father without himself being an adoptive son—for, on the witness of tradition and Scripture, grace-life is the source of adoptive sonship; without the possession of created and uncreated grace such sonship does not and cannot exist. Or to put the same point another way: the act of seeing God face to face in heaven can only eventuate if, as St. Thomas puts it, the divine essence is not only the object seen but also the factor determining the mind to the act of vision. The divine essence must function not only as *id quod videtur* but also as *id quo videtur*.[18]

In other words the self-communication of the triune God is the ontological prerequisite for the beatific vision. Created inherent grace on earth is the guarantee that this self-communication has been achieved—just as, in parallel, the *lumen gloriae* is the guarantee that the act of vision is in progress.

One cannot have a grown-up unless there has first been a child, nor a tree except where previously there has been a seed. Likewise there cannot be glory unless there has first been grace. It may be objected that, absolutely speaking, God could work the miracle of creating an adult or bringing into being a mature tree. Possibly this *is* conceivable—physical laws can be overruled by God's untrammelled might. The case of grace and glory is somewhat different: the bond between them is metaphysical. Not even omnipotence can make a man a father to one who is not his natural or adoptive son—for fatherhood and sonship are correlatives. So too by meta-

18. *Divina substantia non potest videri per intellectum in aliqua specie creata; unde oportet, si Dei essentia videatur, quod per ipsammet essentiam divinam intellectus ipsam videat, ut sic, in tali visione, divina essentia sit et quod videtur et quo videtur* (*C. Gent.* 2.51) — see ST 1a, 12.2 ad 3: ... *divina essentia* ... *per seipsam faciens intellectum in actu* ... (*ibid.*) 5: *ipsa essentia Dei fit forma intelligibilis intellectus* ...."

physical necessity the human mind can see the three-personed God only if it already possesses him, only if he communicates himself through grace.

As to the second tenet, Biel would himself unhesitatingly concede that the possession of sanctifying grace coincides with the possession of the Holy Spirit in person. Now the Holy Spirit is love and holiness together. The communication to man of subsistent love and holiness inevitably betokens his elevation to a state of ontological holiness and worth—to the only holiness and worth that have value for the kingdom of heaven. Without this holiness and worth no human virtue has eternal currency. But this ontological holiness is, by its very nature, incompatible with a state of grave sinfulness. It means descent of God in personal love. Grave sinfulness means rupture with God out of hate.

Grace means that man has passed from a state of enmity to friendship. Grave guilt means a state of enmity towards God. One cannot have it both ways. The same person, at the same time, under the same aspect cannot be both ontologically holy and unholy, both friend and foe of God.

Gathering together: nominalist theology of the supernatural seems to involve this illogicality: God can play father to one who is in no sense his son; he can be seen intuitively by one who, not possessing him, is stripped of the ontological prerequisite for such vision. Man can be at one and the same time God's sworn enemy (not simply through venial selfishness or habitual inclination to self-seeking but through personal, clung-to rebellion) and his staunch friend; at once holy with the essential holiness of deification and unholy through deliberate personal surrender to what is gravely insulting to God.

Chapter 5

We can cover the theology of the supernatural from the sixteenth to the twentieth century within a comparatively brief compass. The reason for the rapidity of our survey is not that these centuries saw only a scanty theological output. Quite the contrary. In the sixteenth, seventeenth and eighteenth centuries dense and massive tomes followed one another from the printing presses of Europe. One thinks of Suarez, Ripalda and John of St. Thomas; of Lessius (1554-1623), Billuart (1685-1757), Sardagna (1731-1775), Tournely (1658-1729)—to mention no others. Later on the manuals of theology began to proliferate.... Rather this phase of scholasticism was, in general, busied with tighter and tighter systematization, with clarification, definition and crystallization of concepts and technical vocabulary. It belongs more specifically to the history of the grace-tract. What is sadly lacking in post-tridentine theology is significant progress in the *dogma* of the supernatural. Instead we encounter the endless speculations of the schools and their ever more and more refined subtleties.

We can list out perhaps six factors that help us to explain the characteristic limitations and narrowness of this period. (I) There was, for example, the solicitude with the scholastic system as such, as though the revealed message of salvation had to be coerced into the mold of this particular theology. (II) There was the eager rivalry of the different theological schools—Thomist, Scotist and Jesuit—among themselves. Each was preoccupied with its own prestige. (III) Moreover Trent, in the very formulae of its chapters and canons, had equivalently canonized the scholastic method and approach—so much so that nominalism quickly became an obsolete and spent force, and Augustinianism an unheard and eccentric voice. Thus the whole enormous vitality of Roman Catholic theology was channeled along severely scholastic lines. This resulted in the tendency to scrutinize and assess every problem that arose according to the criteria of a single system.

(IV) Again, the exigencies of the ever actual controversy with Reformed theologians kept Catholic apologists (e.g., St. Robert Bellarmine, 1542-1621) and theologians (e.g., Suarez, 1548-1617) concentrated on the inherent gift of created, sanctifying grace in order to thwart the Protestant proclamation of declarative justification, extrinsic imputation or the favor of God.

(V) Baius, when he published his unorthodox views, provoked by reaction a tightening of the scholastic synthesis. He was countered with the theory of pure nature—the classical, post-tridentine defense of the supernatural. This hypothesis has continued to haunt and hypnotize scholastic theologians till quite recently. According to Broglie, it constitutes an inevitable explicitation and genuine progress of the aristotelic-thomist system. Nevertheless he rightly observes that, in so far as it is bound up with the particular thomist synthesis which respected Catholic theologians such as Nominalists and Augustinians do not admit, it is not essential to the *dogma* of the supernatural. What is essential to this is the maintaining of the possibility of man's non-vocation to the beatific vision.[1] On the other hand, de Lubac (amidst a *crescendo* of applause from contemporary theologians) dismisses *pure nature* as an artificial construct and as unnecessary, futile even harmful.[2]

(VI) Jansen, with his assertion of irresistible grace and its correlative of a denial of liberty, drove Catholic theologians to a closer inspection of the relationship between grace and freedom. Alongside the struggle against Jansenism there flared up the *de auxiliis* controversy between Dominicans and Jesuits. Actual grace was thus thrust to the center of the theological stage. And so the theology of the supernatural instead of ranging over the spacious, wholesome and enriching domains of divinization and indwelling became cribbed, cabined and confined to the baffling problem of man's liberty and God's efficacious grace. This unfortunate and deleterious shift of accent can be seen mirrored in the dozens of manuals of theology which devoted far too much space to fruitless polemics over actual grace and far too little not only to the indwelling but even to habitual grace. The swing from center to periphery was as complete as it was disastrous for a balanced approach to the supernatural.

Disadvantages

The *disadvantages* of post-tridentine scholasticism seem only too obvious since Vatican II. The supernatural as the self-communication of the triune God, as the personal en-

1. *De fine ultimo humanae vitae* (1948), pp. 184-186; 245-264.
2. de Lubac, *Surnaturel* (1946), recently expanded into two volumes.

counter between God and man was more and more eclipsed. Everywhere dissecting was rife, analyzing, abstracting, speculating and, above all, spinning of subtleties. Natures ousted persons. The supernatural was "thingified." Solicitude with system prevailed. To its adherents it seemed that only the canonized scholastic structure protected the gratuity of the supernatural and that all who opposed it were muddle-headed and confused. Throughout these centuries it is hard to find any ecumenical gesture from the side of Roman Catholic theologians.[3]

To its opponents—and these included, amongst others, all Greek and Protestant theologians—post-tridentine scholasticism seemed to fossilize and desiccate everything it touched. They therefore turned away from it with incomprehension and mistrust. Certainly to a daily increasing number of Roman Catholic theologians, scholasticism appears as irrelevant to modern man. If the dogma of the supernatural is simply what post-tridentine scholasticism presented it as being, they feel that it lacks interest for themselves and for their contemporaries.

Perhaps scholasticism touched its nadir early in the period of our present study—with J. M. de Ripalda (1594-1648). With the prolixity characteristic of this phase of scholasticism he explored the possibility of a *supernatural substance*.[4] Such theorizings, instead of advancing the theology of the supernatural, could only hinder this or lead to a regression. Either

3. See Oskar Garstein, *Rome and the Counter-Reformation in Scandinavia*, Copenhagen (1963).
4. See his *Excellentia entis supernaturalis*, disputatio 23 in volume 1 of *De ente supernaturali disputationes theologicae*, Paris (1870). In this work one meets such phrases as the following: *ipsa substantia supernaturalis esset gratia sanctificans formaliter . . . ; substantia ferens connexionem cum gratia iustificante, aut alio dono supernaturali . . . est intrinsece supernaturalis . . . (ibid.,* sect. 2 n. 6; sect. 3 n. 9).

Ripalda threw the theology of the supernatural back to the early scholastic phase [5] or he betrayed a radical misunderstanding of it. St. Thomas had pointed out centuries before (ST 1a, 2ae, 110.2 ad 2) that the supernatural must be a *relative* concept. God's self-communication is *towards* man. A created *subsistent* supernatural is either an abuse of technical terminology or a basic failure to grasp the implications of man's deification. Hence Ripalda deserves the withering comments that he drew from de Lubac:

> So far as the caliber of his thought goes, it is hardly worth the trouble of fanning its ashes into life.... Verbal criticism, silly suppositions, parade of lofty metaphysics, misleading subtleties, trickster practices with *ad hominem* argumentations, quite shallow grasp of grand, traditional themes, the work of Ripalda exhibits all the symptoms of a theology run to seed. (*Surnaturel*, Paris (1946) pp. 294, 299.)

Advantages

We must not overlook the many *advantages* to the theology of the supernatural that accrued from this phase of scholasticism. During these centuries there arose a considerable number of theologians of the first flight such as Molina (1563-1600),[6] Petavius (1583-1652), Suarez, M. J. Scheeben (1835-1888), to name only a few. Plainly men of such distinction could not dedicate themselves to the ongoing theological

5. See chapter 6. This is the more kindly interpretation.

6. About his famous *Concordia*—published at Lisbon in 1588—Nigel Abercrombie writes: "It would be difficult to name a single treatise of dogmatic theology which has more profoundly affected the history of dogma" (*The Origins of Jansenism*, Oxford [1936], p. 93).

enterprise without enriching it. This indeed happened.

As examples of this enrichment we might cite Suarez's analysis of the friendship between God and man in the union of grace (*Inhabitatio ... per rationem amicitiae—De sanctissimo Trinitatis mysterio* 12, 5.13; Vivès (1856), I, pp. 810-811), or Scheeben's golden pages on the sacramental character and the supernaturality of marriage (*Die Mysterien des Christentums*, sections 84 & 85). Everywhere, too, there was advance in clarification of terms and concepts—e.g.: the notion of the supernatural as against the preternatural or miraculous; the distinctions between efficacious and merely sufficient grace, between *gratia sanans* and *elevans*, between general divine concursus and supernatural grace. The technical instruments of scholastic theology were thus carried to a new pitch of refinement and perfection. The thorny question of the natural desire for the beatific vision was exhaustively canvassed from every angle.[7] Moreover at the close of the nineteenth century there began the significant swing of interest to the theme of the Mystical Body. This has been caught up and developed with alacrity by the twentieth century theologians among whom E. Mersch attained a position of preeminence for his scholarly writings on this theme. The significance of this new trend for the theology of the supernatural can scarcely be exaggerated. It spelt an abandonment of the earlier individualistic approach and a return to an accentuation of its communitarian aspect. The supernatural was thus set where it rightly belongs—in the perspective of the Church and of the sacraments. This immense gain has been assured and canonized by Vatican II. The supernatural is no longer seen as an isolated phenomenon happening to the individual closeted with God. Rather he receives the

7. See Bibliographies in *Gregorianum* 31 (1950), p. 444, note 142 or *Problemi e orientamenti di teologia dommatica*, 2, pp. 545-607.

self-communication of the triune God *in and through* his fellowship in the Mystical Body.

M. de la Taille — K. Rahner

However if we were asked to single out the most impressive development of the theology of the supernatural within the strict boundaries of post-tridentine scholasticism we would unhesitatingly point to the work of M. de la Taille and K. Rahner.[8] These two theologians conducted investigations contemporaneously but independently of one another. Both are set squarely in the thomist tradition; each complements the other. Hence we may treat them together. Their concern is with the interconnection between created and uncreated grace, between sanctifying grace and the indwelling Spirit. They do a real service to the scholastic theology of the supernatural because they offer what appears to us as the sole satisfactory metaphysical explanation of these vital elements of the supernatural. They give a brilliant synthesis of grace and glory, integrating their diverse elements.

De la Taille and Rahner are not, of course, pathfinders in this field. The renewed interest in patristics had forced theologians like Petavius, Scheeben and de Régnon to emphasize once more the importance of the Holy Spirit in any theology of the supernatural. But none of these forerunners succeeded in presenting a convincing theory. Moreover their interest was limited to one aspect only of the supernatural: man's grace-life on earth. They attempted no synthesis of all the elements of the whole realm of the supernatural. Not the least of the merits of de la Taille and Rahner is that they addressed themselves precisely to this task. De la Taille's synthesis covers grace, glory and Hypostatic Union. Rahner does not consider this last. He particularly works from

8. See above, p. 9.

the beatific vision which commands his theology of grace.
We might gather together their ideas in the following form.
We work in broad outlines without stopping to justify each
step in particular. We are not interested in *proving* these
theories but in throwing into relief the insights they contain.

The beatific vision means that man shall see God just as
he is. He is the three-personed God. Therefore in glory man
will see and be united directly with Father, Son and Holy
Spirit. However such vision is metaphysically impossible for
a finite mind unless God himself by his own being determines
the mind of man to this intuitive vision. Nothing created can
achieve this activation of the finite mind—only God himself.
Hence if man is to see Father, Son and Holy Spirit in heaven,
Father, Son and Holy Spirit must give themselves to man first.
This is the ontological prerequisite of vision; this is the grace-
life on earth: the self-communication of the three-personed
God in view of vision; this is why both Scripture and Tradition
present our deification here as *inchoatio formalis gloriae,*
the dawning of what will become the noon-tide of vision.

Our grace-life on earth means (I) *union* between God
and man—how explain this union?; (II) it involves *two*
basic gifts: created and uncreated grace—how explain their
interconnection?

To render an account of the union between the Trinity
and the human person it is not enough to do what many
thomist theologians have been content to do—namely, appeal
to *efficient* causality. Of course in the production of every
union an efficient cause is required in order to bring together the partners to the union and to change what has to
be changed. So in man's deification, the Trinity, working *ad
extra,* brings about the union and causes the created entity
of grace. But we cannot stop short here. More than efficient
causality is at work in man's deification which is, we repeat,

a *union*. Efficiency belongs to extrinsic causality. Efficient cause and effect in no sense coalesce and form one; they are adequately distinct, divided, separated from one another, even pitted against each other. The producing of a union of course requires extrinsic, efficient causality. But the union once established must be explained from within. It is at this point that one must invoke the category of intrinsic causality.

Body and soul, matter and form are the classical intrinsic causes. The hylomorphic union is established and maintained by the mutual self-giving of matter and form—or, better, in the material cause's reception of the formal cause. But can one apply hylomorphic causality to the union between the Trinity and man? The attempt to do so would seem to be fraught with inextricable difficulties. To rate man as the material cause of such a union—therefore, as receiver of God, as being sustained, transformed, elevated, even informed by God would perhaps pose no insuperable difficulty. The problem comes in calling God the formal cause of the union. How can God be equated with a formal cause, seeing that this, in its very act of informing or self-giving, is sustained by and depends on the material cause? In no sense can we admit that God *needs* man. Moreover Trent has defined sanctifying grace as the *sole* formal cause of our justification.[9] This declaration would appear to preclude any denomination of uncreated grace as a formal cause. Finally in hylomorphic union both coefficients are incomplete substances—a downgrading inappropriate whether applied to God or man.

To meet these objections Rahner refers to God as the *quasi-form* of the grace-union. De la Taille's formulation is superior because unequivocal: "created actuation by the uncreated Act." Both mean the same thing. To account for the union they are at one that, over and above efficiency, one

---

9. "Unica formalis causa" — session 6, chapter 7, Denz 1529.

must invoke intrinsic, formal causality—but *analogically*. Both unmistakably ward off from God any taint of lowering or subordinating inherence in the material cause (man). Both safeguard the tridentine affirmation that created grace is the exclusive formal cause. They see it as such because it is a quality inhering in man's substance and so is like any accidental, strictly formal cause. God, by contrast, is of course, no accidental form; he is a quasi-form, an uncreated Act.

At this point we must closely watch how created and uncreated grace are integrated with one another. The deified man stands before the self-giving God as quasi-material cause. God, in his self-communication, is the quasi-formal cause or uncreated Act. Giving himself to man, he receives nothing from man on whom he depends in no wise whatsoever. It is sanctifying grace, the created actuation lodged in man by the advent of the uncreated Act, that is (so to speak) the cementing factor of this union. This created actuation is classified in thomistic metaphysics, according to the analogy of the *last disposition*. A subject about to be "informed" must be made ready for the advent of the new form. In the process of preparation the rôle that is metaphysically speaking decisive falls to the *last disposition*. This stands under the very shadow of the form, with which it is absolutely simultaneous and indissolubly linked. Furthermore, through it is achieved the immediate union of subject and form.

So, analogically speaking, it happens between God and man in deification. Sanctifying grace or created actuation functions as last disposition, making man ready to receive the Trinity or uncreated Act. Man is thus disposed, elevated and braced to bear the stress of God's coming and abiding. The created actuation is simultaneous with the presence of the uncreated Act and is indissolubly bound to this presence. Neither can be there without the other. To say that God has given himself to man, is united with man, is to say that man has undergone real change or has had lodged in him the created actuation. Like every regular last disposition, the created actuation, far from destroying, actually accomplishes the *immediacy* of the union between God and man. It is not erected as a sort of opaque medium or barrier hindering direct contact between the two. On the contrary, it is the metaphysical *raison d'être* and guarantee of the immediacy of the union. Without this created actuation man could not receive God nor be directly joined with him; without it, God could not give himself to man. Like a man's shadow in brilliant sunlight, the created actuation announces that Father, Son and Holy Spirit have entered man's sanctuary in person; it is their seal and signature, the warrant and "anchoring" of their self-communication.

This union of deification is not merely affective, intentional, objective or psychological—as not a few scholastics would have us believe.[10] It is, of course, *also* a union of man's mind and heart with God and it does involve the elevating and enhancing of his knowing and loving capacities. But it contains much more than intentional union; it must not be reduced to a mere psychological resonance in man's being. In fact it is an effective, physical and ontological union. On the other hand, it is not to be interpreted in a pantheistic sense. We speak of a *union* between God and man, not of an identification of man with God, not of a forfeiting of man's individuality, not of his being sunk into, absorbed by or fused with godhead. A real ontological union takes place, with divine substance giving itself to human substance. Nevertheless the union cannot be classed as substantial. It is accidental, hinging on the *accident* of created grace. It is a union *ad agere*, not *ad esse*—i.e, a union wholly geared on the

10. See S. González, "De Gratia" *Sacrae Theologiae Summa*, Madrid (1950), vol. 3, pp. 547-551.

uninterrupted *acts* of knowing and loving God in the beatific
vision. Since it is the ontological presupposition for vision,
since it is intrinsically proportioned and essentially orientated
to vision, it must be characterized by the vision. The circle
is thus completed: we began and we end with vision.

So far as their mechanics are concerned grace here and
glory hereafter run on parallel lines. We have seen how,
through appealing to the analogy of last disposition and its
form, we can gain an integrated view of created and uncreated grace. Moreover we have noted how the created
actuation by the uncreated act in deification goes beyond
man's faculties of knowing and loving and takes place at the
core of his being, in his substance. It constitutes the ontological but *remote* preparation for vision. When a man dies
in the state of deification and is ripe for the vision of God,
a sort of parallel occurs. However, this time it is a question
of *proximate* preparation only: the preparation at depth is
already assured. So now a change is wrought on the level
of the faculties. In order that the intuitive vision of God
may ensue, man's intellect needs its own particular adjust-
ing. This is effected by what is known as the *lumen gloriae*:
a last disposition, a created actuation, equipping, fortifying
and enhancing the intellect so as to be able to receive the
uncreated Act's self-giving addressed precisely to it.

Two particular advantages from the Rahner-de la Taille
approach are noteworthy.

(I) Commonly, in text-book scholasticism, habitual grace
is alleged as the sole and total cause of the state of grace.
Thus indwelling, adoptive sonship, etc. are regarded as the
upshot of grace, as its formal effects. This seems most unsatisfactory and a downgrading of the magnificence of divinization. In fact nothing of the *created* order, no matter how excellent and supernatural, can, of itself, explain the grandeur of
man's deification. The uncreated must be invoked. On the de

la Taille-Rahner view there is a two-fold cause at work: created *and* uncreated grace; created actuation *and* uncreated Act. These two indissolubly interconnected elements of the entitatively supernatural form the combined adequate explanation of all the formal effects of the state of grace: sharing in the divine nature, adoptive sonship, justification, holiness, the splendor of the deified man, his right to the inheritance of the beatific vision. Indeed it is a misunderstanding of the Christian concept of remission of sins to equate it exclusively with the infusion of grace; it is grander than this. It is the descent of the Holy Spirit in person—for he is himself the forgiveness of sins: *ipse est remissio peccatorum* (this fine, ancient and profound phrase, so expressive of the Christian concept of pardon, is found in the former postcommunion of Whit Tuesday. *Proh dolor!* the whole prayer has vanished from the revised, 1970 edition of the Roman Missal).

(II) The first millennium of Christianity heavily underscores the reality of the Holy Spirit in our divinization; the second millennium, or scholasticism, lays stronger stress on created grace. Both these streams of tradition belong to the ever-living Church and enjoy their own rights of citizenship, their own fashion of conveying the *data* of revelation. On the de la Taille-Rahner view these two streams are felicitously brought into confluence. For on this view it does not matter *essentially* (though it might enormously matter *kerygmatically* and *pastorally*) which facet of revelation is highlighted: the uncreated or the created. They are correlatives; each implicates the other; they are joined together by metaphysical ties. *If* God be pleased to communicate himself to a human person, he can do so only by a created actuation. His self-giving is inevitably in and through a created actuation. The created actuation, however, is no free-standing autonomous entity. Its rôle is purely and essentially ancillary. It is there only because God himself is there, only to ensure his immediate presence, only to dispose man for God's self-communication.

Two weaknesses have beset traditional theology of the supernatural: (I) the weakness of not being able to justify metaphysically the created gift of grace. This is the defect of Greek patristic theology and it re-appears in recent theologians such as Scheeben who, rightly, very much want to accentuate the uncreated Gift. (II) The weakness of not being able to give a metaphysical account of the *union* of deification or of allowing uncreated Grace to become a sort of afterthought and upshot of created grace. This is the conspicuous failing of post-tridentine scholasticism. Very neatly and successfully Rahner and de la Taille have side-stepped both these pitfalls. They have thus rendered signal service to scholasticism in general and to the theology of the supernatural in particular. But there remains the vital question which we shall discuss in chapter 7: has any *scholastic* theology of the supernatural relevance for modern man?

Chapter 6 *

SHAPING THE TECHNICAL TERM

THE shaping of the technical term *supernatural* was due to the scholastic theologians. Indeed this term, in its full development, presupposes the aristotelic-thomist system, without which it is hardly intelligible. Hence we fittingly wind up our four long chapters on the scholastic theology of the supernatural with some discussion about genesis and evolution of this word and concept. Part of what is set forth here has already appeared in my article *Supernatural* in the *New New Catholic Encyclopedia*, vol. 13, pp. 812-816.

History

Neither the adjective *supernaturale* nor the adverb *supernaturaliter* was used by classical writers of ancient Rome;

* BIBLIOGRAPHY
Alszeghy, Z., S.J.,
   "Il soprannaturale" *Greg* 31 (1950), pp. 444-448.
Auer, J.,
   "Der Begriff des *Übernatürlichen*" *Die Entwicklung der Gnadenlehre in der Hochscholastik* (1951), zweiter Teil, pp. 229-255.

neither word appears in Lewis and Short's *Latin Dictionary*. However Cicero, Tacitus, Seneca did have equivalent expressions to describe extraordinary *effects*: *divinitus, supra naturam excedens*.

The corresponding Greek adjective: ὑπερφυές is used by classical authors for *overgrown, enormous, monstrous, extraordinary, marvellous*. Likewise the adverb: ὑπερφυως is common enough for *wonderfully, exceedingly*.

One searches in vain for the word in the NT, in the ancient texts of the Liturgy or in the patristic writings of the first centuries.[1] Ripalda (ob. 1648) criticized the theologians of his day for saying that the word *supernatural* was not to be found among the Fathers of the Church (*perperam aiunt recentes scriptores nusquam apud Patres vocem supernaturalitatis inveniri in De ente supernaturali* lib. 1, disp. 1. sect. 3, n. 20, Paris, 1870, p. 4). From the Greek Fathers he picked out a few passages which he cited according to subsequent *Latin translations* carrying the word *supernaturalis*. He therefore completely failed to make his point.

Bainvel, J. V.,
  "La constatation du surnaturel" *Nature et Surnaturel*, 4th ed (1911), pp. 293-326.
Bouillard, H.,
  i) *Conversion et grâce chez s. Thomas d'Aquin*, especially, pp. 203-207.
  ii) "L'idée de surnaturel et le mystère chrétien" *L'homme devant Dieu*, Paris (1964), tome 3, pp. 153-166.
de Broglie, V., S.J.,
  De fine ultimo humanae vitae, Paris (1948), especially, pp. 126-162.
Deneffe, A., S.J.,
  "Geschichte des Wortes *supernaturalis*" *Z Kath Th* 46 (1922), pp. 337-360.

---

1. See e.g., E. J. Goodspeed, *Index Patristicus sive Clavis Patrum Apostolicorum Operum*, Leipzig (1907).

Under the pen of the Greek Neoplatonists, *supernatural* began to take on the meaning of superior substance. St. Proclus of Constantinople (ob. 446) and, more important, his disciple Pseudo-Dionysius (*c.* 500) head a long tradition of labelling *supernatural* all spiritual beings, especially God but also angels and even the human soul.

In a famous text, St. Cyril of Alexandria (ob. 444), breaking up the adjective into its components of noun and preposition, gets very close to the modern notion of the strictly supernatural—a fact that is not surprising when one recalls the exceptional richness of Cyril's theology of grace. Treating of our adoptive sonship, he presents it as our elevation through Christ to a dignity surpassing not only *human* nature but Nature "tout court": εἰς τὸ ὑπὲρ φύσιν ἀξίωηα διὰ χριστὸν. The summons to the supernatural is to something beyond nature: πρὸς τὰ ὑπὲρ φύσιν. Contrasted with us is Christ: his endowments are natural: κατὰ φύσιν (*In Ioann.* 1.12; PG 73.153 B-D; cf. *Dial 4 de ss. Trinit.* PG 75.882.C. About Christ, Cyril affirms that his divine nature won recognition from the *supernatural splendor* of his works: ἐκ τῆς τῶν κατω-

Landgraf, A. M.,
"Die Sprache der frühscholastischen Theologie," "Die Erkenntnis des Übernatürlichen" *Dogmengeschichte der Frühscholastik* (1952), 1/1 pp. 20-29; 141-201.

de Lubac, H.,
i) "Remarques sur l'histoire du mot surnaturel" *Nouv Rev Th* 61 (1934), pp. 225-249; 350-370.
ii) *Surnaturel*, Paris (1946), pp. 323-428.
(N. B. R. Leys, S.J., joins issue with de Lubac's treatment of *supernatural* in Gregory of Nyssa: *L'image de Dieu chez s. Grégoire de Nyssa* (1951), pp. 98-106.
iii) "Nature humaine et surnaturel" *Athéisme et sens de l'homme* (1968), pp. 96-112.

Terrien, J. B., S.J.,
"Du caractère surnaturel et gratuit des dons faits par Dieu à ses enfants..." *La grâce et la gloire*, Paris (1901), vol. 2, pp. 327-368.

ϱεωμένων ὑπερφυὸυς λαμπρότητος, *Dial 7 de ss. Trinit.* PG 75.1116.B. St. Basil, in his treatise on the Holy Spirit, uses ὑπερφυές of the love displayed towards men by the Father in giving his Son on account of our sins. He describes this divine love as something grand and surpassing: μέγα τι καὶ ὑπερφυές. Though Basil is hardly using this term technically, he seems to give it a content and extension that bring it close to the later *Fachausdruck*: *supernatural—De Spiritu sancto,* 14.32 PG 32.124.C).

In the ninth century, through translations of the works of pseudo-Dionysius made principally by John Scotus Erigena (c. 850) *supernatural* made its *début* in the theology of the West. It has the neoplatonist sense of superior being. For Scotus Erigena God is the supreme *supernatural* nature causing all else to pale into insignificance: ... *vilescit omnis creatura visibilis et invisibilis, dum comparatur summae et supernaturali naturae* ... (*Expos. super Ierarchiam caelestem,* 2, 3; PL 122. 154.A). In a similar sense, Mary is invoked as *Regina supernaturalis* (PL 96.288.D).

Despite the promise of a great future which the writings of Scotus Erigena held for the development of *supernatural,* it was not till the thirteenth century and St. Thomas that the word was launched into theological circulation as a technical term. Landgraf is emphatic on this point: it is an incontestable fact of history (he asserts) that up to the thirteenth century, *supernatural* is never once used unequivocally (*op. cit.,* p. 141. He is supported by Auer, *op. cit.,* p. 230). In the thirteenth century its use became more and more frequent, its meaning less and less vague; it crystallized as a technical term above all through the genius of St. Thomas. St. Albert the Great (ob. 1280) seldom used *supernaturalis* in his commentary on the Sentences (completed before 1250). But in his later *Summa theologiae* (after 1270), where he had markedly undergone the influence of his peerless disciple

Thomas, he employed *supernaturalis* repeatedly—but in the broad sense of the divine, what is willed by God, what is bound up with God (Auer, *op. cit.*, p. 236). To express the supernatural, St. Bonaventure favors such phrases as *super statum naturae, super terminum naturae.* Matthew of Aquasparta, O.F.M. (ob. 1302) echoes these and adds to them a formula beloved of St. Thomas: *supra proportionem naturae.* Indeed he is deeply indebted to St. Thomas. In dealing with grace *supernaturalis* comes often from his pen. For example, discussing grace as a created reality he uses *supernaturalis* 21 times and in the thomistic sense (Auer, *op. cit.*, pp. 241-242). Scotus employs *supernaturalis* often and in various senses (*ibid.*, p. 249).

As we have said, St. Thomas is above all the shaper of the technical concept. He himself is enamored of the word. Thus in a single article of his *De veritate* (12.7) one can count upwards of twenty usages. Sometimes he employs the term in its neoplatonist acceptation. Thus he presents the beatific vision as a contemplation of *supernatural* Truth where modern theology would prefer: *subsistent* Truth (*contemplatio patriae, qua supernaturalis veritas per essentiam videtur* (ST 2a, 2ae, 5.1, ad 1) and God as the *supernatural* principle of our faith (*ibid.*, 6.1). Far more commonly (a complete tally would hardly be feasible without the aid of an electronic computer) St. Thomas applies *supernatural* not to superior *substances* but to surpassing *effects*.

However only in the last three centuries has the word reached the first flight of importance as a technical term. Evidence for this assertion can be had by glancing through the indices of the editions of the Fathers, or of the medieval theologians. The word hardly appears. Not till Pius V's condemnation of the 21st and 23rd propositions of Baius in 1567 (Denz 1921, 1923) did the magisterium officially adopt it. Its apotheosis came in 1870 when Vatican I embodied it for the first time in a conciliar decree (Denz 3004, 3005, 3006, 3008).

Technical term

If one scans closely the phenomena listed in a modern dictionary under *supernatural,* one will remark that they fall into one of two classes: I) superior *substances,* II) surpassing *effects.*

The first class bears witness to the persistence in popular circles of the Greek tradition which was also the prevalent theological usage up to the thirteenth century. As we saw, it crops up in St. Thomas, although it is especially the weight of his authority that swings the scales in favor of the second class. Henceforward this latter predominates in theological literature. From it develops the strictest technical sense. However even after St. Thomas the first class keeps on rallying support. It recurs frequently among the mystics of the fourteenth century. In the seventeenth century it flares up in a sort of sickly brilliance with Ripalda's theory of the *supernatural substance,* which theologians showed their good sense by rebutting.

As we understand it, the strictest acceptation of supernatural does not exactly square with either of the two classes above. It borrows from each, perhaps, but is a concept far richer in meaning than either.

In the strictest, technical sense, then, supernatural does *not* mean (I) superior substances like angels or God taken in their lofty isolation, invisibility and absoluteness; *nor* does it mean (II) merely wonderful, surpassing effects like miracles and prodigies. Rather it is reserved to signify a new relationship of man to God, a fresh contact between Infinite and finite, a real descent of God to a personal creature.

Nature

In order to penetrate more deeply the meaning of this notion, we must pause over the correlatives of the supernatural, i.e., *nature* and *natural*.

The technical theology of the supernatural was bound to remain stunted until a satisfactory philosophy of nature had been evolved. This was achieved thanks to St. Albert the Great and St. Thomas, under the aegis of Aristotle. Prethomistic writers like Anselm, Bernard and Peter Lombard fight shy of the word *supernatural*, largely because of the inadequacies of their philosophy of nature.

Nature, before being established by the scholastic theologians as antithesis to *supernatural*, had gone through three main stages of historical growth. They may be rapidly and roundly sketched in as follows:

(I) Greek, especially aristotelic, philosophy conceived Nature and the universal laws springing from the inflexible essences of things as the sole and peremptory norm for every happening in the world. God was regarded either as wholly aloof from the world, or as producing it according to inexorable necessity. Contemplating the beauty of Nature and its unswerving regularity, God might display a certain olympian complacency; but never might he show towards individual men the slightest trace of selective, personal love. Such a philosophy, precluding in principle the very possibility of the supernatural, was radically pagan and anti-Christian.

(II) Realizing the need to remedy this deep defect, St. Augustine went to the opposite extreme. He refused to define natures by reference to the inexorable laws of fixed essences. Instead he reduced natures to what God wants things to be, to the mere objects of God's good pleasure (... *voluntas tanti*

utique conditoris conditae rei cuiusque natura sit—Civ. 21.8.2
CSEL p. 531). He broke definitively with ancient naturalism.
Nature as understood by the pagans of the past became trans-
muted into the *creation* of Christian theology:

. . . *id enim erit cuique rei naturale quod ille fecerit a quo est omnis modus, numerus, ordo naturae* (*C. Faust.* 26.3; CSEL p. 731).	that will be according to each thing's nature what he made from whom all shape, multiplicity and arrangement of nature comes.

In fact Augustine was not greatly interested in natures, taken
in isolation. In that sense Albert the Great justly criticized
him: "he did not understand natures well" (*non bene scivit
naturas*). Augustine is always a theologian and a man of
God. His interest is in the origin or the end of natures. He
studies them as they issue from God or as they go to him . . . .
Or he sees them as wholly bathed in and sustained by the
creative love of God.[2]

Giving everything to God, Augustine readily accounted
for miracles and for God's personal intervention in the world.
But his approach labors under serious drawbacks. If created
natures are not stable principles of action possessed of intrinsic necessity, it is difficult to establish any coherent metaphysics, to admit secondary causes and draw deductions from
their workings, to afford any basis for the natural sciences in
so far as they rely on the uniformity of nature. Moreover on
the augustinian hypothesis it would be impossible to draw
a firm line of demarcation between ordinary and extraordinary
(miraculous) events.

Plainly voluntarism, if allowed to become extreme, is
beset by weakness. Common sense seems to proclaim that

2. See H. de Lubac, *Le mystère du surnaturel* (1965), pp. 41-45.

things are endowed with some internal principle of stability. We see such an understanding of nature when St. Basil the Great (ob. 379) affirms that the *nature* of water cannot explain the effects of baptism, that the angels are not holy by *nature* (for if they were they would not differ from the Holy Spirit) or that no man is a slave by *nature* (*De Spiritu sancto* 15.35; 16.38; 20.51 PG 32. 132.A; 136-137; 160.D). Vatican II endorses this insight of common sense when it declares that all things, by the very circumstance of their having been created, are endowed with their own stability, truth, goodness, proper laws and order (*Gaudium et spes* 36).

(III) St. Albert and above all St. Thomas laid down the *via media* between the rigid, self-enclosed naturalism of the Greeks and the voluntarism of Augustine. On the one hand they admitted that natures are abiding principles of activity endowed with internal necessity;[3] on the other, they denied that nature contained the clues to the understanding of the whole range of reality. The personal God, in the initiative of sheer love, could always enter onto the stage of history, transcending the demands of nature and outstripping its forces. Thus was forged a philosophy of nature consonant with the demands of Christian revelation. A landmark had been attained. The systematic theology of the supernatural was able to advance.

Various senses of nature

Supernatural evokes *natural* which in its turn evokes nature. We need to note a quartet of senses for *nature/natural* because they all bear, though unequally, on *supernatural*.

3. See Bouillard, *Conversion et grâce*, pp. 87 & 205; also discussion by Seckler, *op. cit.*, pp. 197-220.

(I) *genetic sense*: what is given with nature from the start, or belongs to one from one's birth; the endowments of one's origin, even though some of these may in fact be transcendent. In this sense, common in early Church documents, man is considered not philosophically but historically, i.e., according to the condition of his actual creation. Thus Adam's original justice was *natural*.[4] Original sin was a wound inflicted on human nature.[5]

(II) *specific, abstract sense*: the ontological type communicable to many; the sheaf of essential attributes leaving out of count their realization in individuals. The value of this abstract concept calls for comment owing to recent controversies centering on the supernatural. In order to demonstrate the gratuity of the supernatural, the classical, post-tridentine scholastic procedure has been to appeal to the hypothetical state of pure nature where man would exist fully equipped with all natural resources and end, but shorn of any supernatural influence whatsoever. Certain modern thinkers[6] challenged such a procedure as futile: proving the gratuity of the supernatural in a state of pure nature does not prove

4. See Augustine, *Spir. et litt.* 24.47: *Hoc enim agit spiritus gratiae, ut imaginem Dei, in qua naturaliter facti sumus, instauret in nobis;* Leo, *Sermo* 12.1, PL 54, 168 C: . . . *naturalem nostri generis dignitatem.* But cf. *Sermo* 28.3, PL 54. 223.A: *naturalis generatio* where the meaning veers off to something else. See also Denz 239, 389, 396. As a rule, however, the second Council of Orange (529) and the men of the sixth century in general, contrasted nature and grace much as they did man and God. Nature belonged to man's orbit and grace to God's (see Denz 370-400). In those days men did not think in terms of two orders: natural and supernatural. They saw every intervention of God as inspired by and expressive of his gratuitous love.

5. See Denz 371, 400.

6. Cf. *Le Mystère du Surnaturel,* RechScRel 36 (1949), pp. 80-121.

its gratuitousness in the present order where man, intrinsically affected by the supernatural, is necessarily totally other than he would be in any such phantom state. This attitude, while showing an excellent appreciation of the deep, inward resonance in man evoked by his call to the beatific vision, does not do equal justice to the abstractive power of the intellect with its ability to shape a single concept valid for human nature wheresoever found or howsoever postulated. For the supernatural, no matter how inwardly and deeply it influences and transforms human nature, cannot change it substantially but only accidentally. The example of sex is instructive: its influence is far-reaching and intrinsic; the differences between men and women are not only anatomical and physiological but also emotional and psychological. Yet the differences of sex are accidental, not substantial; and the abstract concept of human nature fits both men and women perfectly. Similarly, the destination of man to a natural and commensurate, as against a supernatural and surpassing goal or *vice versa* leaves the abstract concept of human nature untouched. However (as we shall see in chapter 7) such a line of argument, while it may carry weight for past thinkers, fails to convince moderns emancipated from scholastic bondage.

(III) *individual senses*: e.g., human nature of Christ. If there is little difficulty in forming an abstract concept of human nature, it is another matter when one tries to fashion a satisfactory concept of human nature in the individual. The shadow of the supernatural lies across this path. The concept of concrete human nature must be built up from various sources: sensation, intelligence, self-consciousness and history (this illustrates the forces and resiliency of a concretely existing nature). The fact that the last page of human history has yet to be written suggests a certain incompleteness—which

may not be serious. However what is more troubling is the
fact that the lives of all men have been led in a supernatural
order; this has wrapped man around like the air he breathes
and has affected him within and without. Hence when one
studies existing human nature, one studies it as somehow
supernaturalized. But to know the supernatural as such and
delineate it against the natural is beyond unaided reason.
Revelation is needed.

(IV) *cosmic sense*: the universe and everything in it—Nature
with a capital N. However, different senses are attached to
Nature according as one is a physicist or a metaphysician.,
The former limits Nature to the sense-perceptible; the latter
extends it to embrace the whole gamut of creation, the spiritual
as well as the sensory. When the theologian speaks of the
supernatural as transcending the demands of Nature he means
Nature in the metaphysical sense.

In order to clarify further the supernatural in its strictest
technical sense we must pause over three statements about it:

A — it involves something infinitely more precious than mira-
cles or preternatural gifts;
B — it connotes with metaphysical necessity a created gift;
C — it surpasses all the demands and forces of Nature.

Miracle

A — A miracle (called by some authors *supernaturale
quoad modum*) e.g., the sudden mending of a shattered bone,
restores a perfectly *natural* gift of health. The wonder of it
lies sheerly in the instantaneousness of the recovery—attri-
butable only to an almighty Cause. In the present order
miracles are linked with the strictly supernatural—but in the

lowly capacity of handmaids. No miracle is wrought (teaches St. Thomas) except in some connection with grace and glory (*per aliquos supernaturales effectus, qui miracula dicuntur, in aliquam supernaturalem cognitionem credendorum homo adducitur* ... — ... *id propter quod miracula fiunt: scilicet ad manifestandum aliquid supernaturale* ... — S Th 2a, 2ae, 178.1 *in corpore* and ad 3. Note St. Thomas' elastic use of *supernaturalis* in these quotations). The miracle plays its important but subordinate rôle in the supernatural scene: the overwhelming transformation that "explodes" before our eyes symbolizes the marvelous transformations wrought in the hidden recesses of the soul through the strictly supernatural.

Preternatural

A *preternatural* gift (sometimes listed as *supernaturale relativum*) is one which, though unowed and therefore gratuitous, nevertheless perfects a nature within the range of nature's own perfectibility. The bodily immortality that scholasticism attributes to Adam is cited as an example. Bodily immortality means prolongation of man's natural being; however it comes gratuitously to a composite being naturally liable to decay. According to thomistic doctrine, preternatural gifts spring from grace, which is strictly supernatural. Consequently the grace-endowed man has within him the seed of fleshly immortality. While a preternatural gift is bound up with the strictly supernatural, nevertheless it falls far below it in excellence.

Created gift

B — This point has been already discussed in chapters 1 and 3. Hence we can be quite brief here. As the supernatural spells a new descent of God to a creature, bringing

about a new relationship and contact, it clearly gives birth
to a new union. Now the very reality of this union exacts,
with metaphysical necessity, some real change somewhere.
Such change is unthinkable in God (Jm 1:17). Therefore it
must be in the creature (cf. *C. gent.* 3.51). But what is received in the creature must itself be created. Hence unless
we are prepared to admit some created gift lodged in the
creature we jeopardize the very reality of the supernatural.

The created gift is the foundation of a new relationship
between God and the human person. In one sense it may be
described as absolute for it is a quality inhering in the creature. In another sense however it is relative—in so far as it
is the foundation of a real relation (*relatio realis*) of the
creature to God. The relation of God to the creature is, on
the contrary, only one of reason (*relatio rationis*: the immutability of God forces us to adopt this position). The in-
equality of these relations (*real* from the creature's side
towards God, *logical only* from God's side towards the creature) makes no special difficulty for the supernatural, for
it is often paralleled elsewhere, e.g., in the relationship existing between Creator and creature, the Word and his human
nature, Mary and the Word-made-Flesh: on her side the
mother-son reference is real; on his (according to Sts. Thomas,
Bonaventure and a host of others) it is logical only.

Beyond claims and forces

C – The supernatural surpasses all the demands and
forces of Nature. This is a complex assertion. It means, first,
that the supernatural is unowed or gratuitous. A grasp of this
typically scholastic concept of the *unowed* is best gained
by considering what is *owed* to the particular nature of man.
Human nature needs body and soul—these are structurally
owed (*constitutive debita*); spiritual and sensory faculties of

action—these are consequently owed (*consecutive debita*) for without them man's nature would be nonsensically crippled; outside aids such as providence, divine concursus, proportioned goal, appropriate sanctions and rewards for right behavior (*exigitive debita*). In none of these senses is the supernatural owed to nature. Casting this in parallel phraseology we say that the supernatural surpasses all nature's demands and forces.

Secondly, not only is the supernatural unowed to the *particular* nature of man, exceeding all his exigencies, it is likewise unowed to the whole of created Nature exceeding all its exigencies. The carving of a *Moses* is beyond the capacities of the block of marble out of which it was hewn by Michelangelo. Nevertheless it is not supernatural. It is well within the scope of Michelangelo's genius. The supernatural surpasses not only the capacities of every individual creature even of an archangel; it further surpasses the powers of the aggregate of all created natures and of the Cosmos itself. Indeed it exceeds not only all actual creatures and creation but also all conceivably possible creatures and creations. Nothing created nor "creatable" can be thought of that the supernatural does not outstrip.

Thirdly, as has been repeatedly pointed out, the supernatural implies a new relationship, a fresh contact between God and man, a divine descent and union with a creature. Therefore in the very concept of the supernatural in this strictest technical sense is implied the pre-existence of its term and of the Universe. Man cannot be elevated to the supernatural unless he exists. This does not necessarily mean that a time-interval must separate man's creation from his elevation. Both may take place simultaneously. But creation enjoys a priority of order; unless one respects this, one makes man's elevation unintelligible.

Now, just as man's particular creation logically forestalls

his supernatural elevation, so *a fortiori* the general creation of the Universe anticipates everything supernatural. Of course, without the pre-existence of this world, man himself cannot be imagined: he is essentially an inhabitant requiring a habitat. But seeing that the creation of the world itself is presupposed to the supernatural, its creation cannot properly be described as supernatural—and this despite the fact that its creation manifestly exceeds its own demands and forces. If then earlier writers like St. Bonaventure (1221-1274) describe creation as *supernaturalis mutatio* (*In Sent*. 2, d. 1, p, 1, a. 1 q. 2, concl. ad 1) they are employing the term in a broader sense where any effect whose unique cause is God can be so styled. The supernatural, being a relative notion, has to take for granted the existence of men, angels and the Cosmos—as much as it has to presuppose the existence of God.

Fourthly, the supernatural surpasses both exigencies and forces *taken together*. *Exigencies*: the creation of a human soul is beyond the reach of creatures; nevertheless it is natural; because it is necessarily joined with the procreation of a human body; nature demands the soul's creation and infusion. *Forces*: a particular personal choice is outside natural exigencies; yet it is natural, because it is the upshot of the normal resources of a being endowed with free-will.

These remarks, together with the clarifications running through earlier chapters, should abundantly illustrate the full force of *supernatural* as it was presented in chapter 1 of this work.

Chapter 7

TEILHARD DE CHARDIN AND THE TWENTIETH CENTURY
THEOLOGY OF THE SUPERNATURAL [1]

PART I: *Teilhard and his vision*

A characteristic of mid twentieth century theology of the
supernatural is its spirited and mounting reaction against
scholasticism, especially in the last or post-tridentine phase.
This reaction has long roots. One of its unwitting initiators
was assuredly Maurice Blondel (1861-1949) with his important doctoral thesis: *L'action* (1893). It is associated with
many famous names (e.g., Henri de Lubac, S.J.), who—be
it noted—addresses his criticisms exclusively to the later
scholastics and remains a staunch and erudite admirer of St.
Thomas. Fr. Eugene Hillman, C.S.Sp. refers to "the stormy
controversies, dramatically associated with Henri de Lubac's
return to the authentic Christian tradition in *Surnaturel*" and

1. This chapter first appeared in the pages of *The Australasian
Catholic Record* 58 (1971) and 59 (1972). It is reprinted with the
gracious permission of the Editor.

he rightly adds that this work "finally set in order the relationship between the natural and the supernatural." [2]

Undoubtedly the central personality of this reaction is Pierre Teilhard de Chardin, S.J. (1881-1955). As perhaps no other twentieth century thinker, Teilhard has caught the attention of the serious-minded reader of every class, creed and country. In the eyes of many he is a prophet of the modern age.

So far as the public is concerned, Teilhard's force as a writer has been greatly assisted by his personality and his appearance (he was decidedly photogenic). He was a man of rare and aristocratic charm, of versatile culture, of exceptional courage (for which he was officially decorated in World War I). No one can fail to admire the steadfastness of his commitment to the Church and his Order, in the teeth of persistent and most anguishing trials. He had a genius for friendship and was a traveler of vast experience.

Teilhard's publications fall into two classes—professional and non-professional. The first forms quite a sizable corpus, as may be seen by consulting the "bibliographie des oeuvres de Teilhard de Chardin" listed by Claude Cuénot: *Teilhard de Chardin—a biographical Study*.[3] This first group is strictly scientific. Teilhard was first and foremost a geologist who branched into pre-history and thence into palaeontology. He earned for himself an enviable international reputation and was accorded membership in his country's Legion of Honor. Teilhard's professional output has no direct bearing on the theology of the supernatural. So it need not detain us. However one fact should be registered: the very existence of the professional publications forbids the dismissal of the non-

2. *The Wider Ecumenism*, London (1968), p. 65.
3. Translated into English by V. Colimore, London (1965), pp. 409-482.

professional as airy flights of an eccentric and poetic imagination, especially since the chief of these were the flower of his most mature and intense reflection.

The public at large knows Teilhard only from his non-professional works. These appeared posthumously, headed by *The Phenomenon of Man* published in France in 1955 (*Le phénomène humain*). It represents the epitome of his genial vision. Although a work neither of technical theology nor by a professional theologian, this book is of the first importance for the theology of the supernatural. It attains this eminence not only because of the positive, constructive contribution it makes in this area of theology, but also because of the challenge it flings down, of the questions it raises. The far-reaching implications of these have yet to be measured. One thing is certain: Teilhard has shaken the structure of neo-scholasticism to its foundations. Moreover he has caused a somersaulting in Roman Catholic circles of theology comparable with the revolution headed by Galileo (1564-1642) four centuries ago in the field of physical sciences. Naturally Teilhard has drawn on himself the fire of the veteran scholastics as indeed of all who (in his phrase) are unable to "renounce the comfort of familiar narrowness." [4]

The range of his interests and allusions, his abundant usage of the vocabulary of modern science make Teilhard difficult reading for the uninitiated. However, this drawback is compensated for by the vigor and freshness of his style (mercifully stripped of the technicalities of scholasticism), by its poetic quality and occasional lyricism,[5] above all, by the

4. *The Phenomenon of Man*, Fontana Books (1969), p. 249.

5. Cuénot, *op. cit.*, p. 42 writes: "His quality as a poet is shown in the astonishing rhythms of *La puissance spirituelle de la matière, La messe sur le monde* .... His lyric works rank with the finest of the world's religious poetry."

limpidity and power of his insights. Perhaps his greatest attribute is his ability to synthesize.

Teilhard was a man of integrated personality. There was nothing schizophrenic or departmentalized about him. He was not a priest on Sunday and a scientist on Monday. Always he was a priest and scientist, believer and savant. His science forced him to his knees in adoration just as his priesthood fed his unwearying zest for research, field-work and contact with his fellows.[6] In *The Phenomenon of Man* he aimed at harmonizing the data of science with the data of revelation. In the cosmic pole of the evolutionary process disclosed by modern investigators and in the Christ proclaimed by St. Paul, Teilhard discerned first a correspondence, then a parity and lastly an identity. He invested Christ with cosmogenetic dimensions so that cosmic convergence meant "Christic" emergence.

Besides being priest and scientist, Teilhard was a poet and a mystic who loved his fellow men and the whole world (not only spiritual but also material).[7] He had not the slightest desire to escape from the world. Rather he consistently sought to find Christ in it and to build on earth the Kingdom of God. He was an irrepressible optimist, unbalked even by two World Wars. Because the evolutionary upthrust was tilted infallibly onwards to Christ, it had to triumph. Teilhard saw life, man, evolution—all as swept along in the triumph of Christ.

To many readers, Vatican II's *Pastoral Constitution on the Church in the World Today* seems an endorsement of

6. See Teilhard's papers in *Science and Christ*, London (1968), pp. 187-191; 199-205; 214-220—good summaries of the ideals that animated him.

7. See "Hymne à la matière," *Hymne de l'univers*, Editions du Seuil (1961), pp. 111-115.

Teilhard's vision. Certainly the Council acknowledges the shift from a static to a dynamic and evolutionary approach to reality (*Gaudium et spes,* n. 5); it significantly shuns scholastic terminology; it makes no mention of the *two orders* so dear to post-tridentine scholastics; it insists that the Christian must serve God in the world of today and construct the City of God not by a flight from the world but by living in it and helping it; it voices a thoroughly teilhardian optimism; it constantly takes for granted a certain proportion between earthly and human affairs on the one hand and on the other the supernatural last end to which man is called in the mystery of Christ.[8]

Teilhard's vision

Teilhard's thinking is commanded by Sacred Scripture. He drew from St. John and St. Paul his understanding of the cosmic rôle of Christ and of the Incarnation. This mystery he accepted as an unassailable fact of history with which in his view every scientist, indeed every individual had to reckon. Teilhard also took his stand on the findings of science whose significance he elucidated with masterly penetration. He *saw* the depth in time behind us,[9] the convergence ahead, the infinitesimally small, the colossally great, mind-staggering interstellar space, the proliferation of life, "the amazing profusion of organic matter" with its "matted complexity" (*The Phenomenon of Man,* p. 86), the majestic rhythms of duration ("perception... de la Lenteur" *Le phénomène humain,* p. 283). He admitted a space-time continuum involving billions of years.

From the well-known progressive series: crystallization,

8. See de Lubac, *Athéisme et sens de l'homme* (1968), pp. 120-121.
9. "... by means of the remarkable phenomena of sedimentation and

macromolecules, viruses, living cells, their clustering first into colonies, next into organisms, the mounting complication of the nervous system.... Teilhard abstracted his law of complexity-consciousness, the very formulation of his vision. Reality develops towards complexity and converges towards consciousness. Evolution is characterized by its forward tilt in the direction of greater complexity and consciousness; in the direction of hominization; finally in the direction of Christ and the plenitude of Christ. The law of complexity-consciousness is grounded on the *without* and the *within* of things. Besides its material aspect or its *without*, everything has also its psychic or spiritual face or its *within* [10]—though in fact this might escape our techniques of measurement. The former is the basis for complexification, the latter for convergence.

Teilhard saw a single evolutionary process at work, spiralling upwards along a privileged axis, generating, as it went, earth, organized matter, life, consciousness, reflection. According to him the upward thrust of the evolutionary process did not halt with man who therefore may in no sense be dismissed as a fortunate anomaly, a chance outcrop, a brief epiphenomenon in the vast processes of Nature. On the contrary: man is the chief target of evolution which, with his advent, becomes self-conscious. God hands over to man the reins of its control.[11] Man "the last-born, the freshest, the

fossilization we can trace the biological past of this planet over a period of nearly a thousand million years," Teilhard, *The Future of Man*, Fontana Books (1969), p. 303.

10. See e.g., *The Future of Man* (1969), p. 135.

11. "One may say that until the coming of Man it was a natural selection that set the course of morphogenesis and cerebration, but that after Man it is the power of invention that begins to grasp the evolutionary reins," Teilhard (1950), *The Future of Man* (1969), p. 307.

most complicated, the most subtle of all the successive layers of life" becomes "the arrow pointing the way to the final unification of the world in terms of life" (*The Phenomenon of Man*, p. 247). It is for man to organize and unify humanity. This is to be achieved by conscious collaboration with Christ in building up the body of Christ.

Although Teilhard sees the vast evolutionary movement in a slow march towards Christ, he does not for one moment delude himself with the idea that cosmic evolution and hominization could *of themselves* cause the incarnation and exact the supernatural. These can come only from on high as the wholly free and transcendent intervention of the Father of mercies.[12]

Teilhard admits only one, overriding evolutionary drive. At the same time he insists that within this single process one must distinguish certain *jumps*. When complexity and convergence reach a particular pitch of ripeness, a metamorphosis occurs, a critical threshold is crossed, a new order begins; there is a qualitative change, a re-birth to a new dimension of being. The biosphere is the upshot of one such critical threshold. Once unleashed, life continuously evolves, complexifies, concentrates. This is particularly remarkable in the field of cerebralisation (*The Phenomenon of Man*, p. 161): it is here that mind emerges. In its turn consciousness, when released, keeps on evolving, ripening and gathering towards a new critical threshold: reflection in man. Across the ages, man changes little morphologically;[13] but his brain is constantly

12. See quotations and comments of H. de Lubac, *Athéisme et sens de l'homme* (1968), pp. 130-141.

13. "Du point de vue ostéologique, sur cet intervalle (30,000 years) pas de coupure appréciable le long du phylum humain;—et même, jusqu'à un certain point, aucun changement *majeur* dans les progrès de sa ramification somatique" (*Le phénomène humain*, p. 223).

developing. Whereas in the biosphere the unit of life is the cell, and the thrust of evolution is in the clustering and complexifying of cells—now, in the noosphere, the unit is the person and the thrust of evolution is in spiritual synthesis or towards greater inter-personal communion of men and the gathering of them together in communities and all-embracing societies. Teilhard has unbounded confidence in what can be achieved by men through team work: "...nothing in the universe can resist the converging energies of a sufficient number of minds sufficiently grouped and organized" ("The Spiritual Repercussions of the Atom Bomb," *The Future of Man,* p. 149).

Teilhard's vision can be summed up in his own words:

If the world is convergent and if Christ occupies its center, then the Christogenesis of St. Paul and St. John is nothing else and nothing less than the extension, both awaited and unhoped for, of that noogenesis in which cosmogenesis—as regards our experience—culminates (*The Phenomenon of Man,* p. 325).

During his last years he endured the throes of frustration because he was consistently forbidden to publish what he believed was the truth, essentially Christian truth. However his courage did not flag, and he was buoyed up by the conviction "that a truth once seen, even by a single mind, always ends up by imposing itself on the totality of human consciousness." [14]

His ladder of cosmogenesis runs thus: geogenesis, biogenesis, psychogenesis, noogenesis, Christogenesis. At once

14. *Ibid.,* p. 241; cf. Pensée L, *Hymne de l'univers* (1961), pp. 183-184.

one observes that for Teilhard realities are not objects but processes; *being* and *essence* yield place to *becoming* and *genesis;* the end holds pride of place—without it nothing has meaning or existence. Without Christ, there is neither consistency nor intelligibility.

This bald and sketchy account of Teilhard's vision suffices for our purposes. Plainly Teilhard's position, if able to be upheld, sounds the death-knell to a particular brand of scholasticism. Plainly also it is portentous with consequence for the theology of the supernatural.

PART II: *The case against scholasticism* [15]

What a genius contributes is above all a new insight. The arguments he marshals to support this may be more or less defective. For insight is not measured by dexterity in ratiocination. Scientists, philosophers and theologians have scrutinized arguments that Teilhard has advanced, and they have sometimes found them wanting.[16] His vision of reality, however, has been acclaimed by thousands all over the world. It is his vision, not his argumentation, that interests us—his vision in so far as it bears on the theology of the supernatural. Perhaps we can best draw out the implications of his vision by demonstrating what it rejects in the scholastic theology of the supernatural and the reason for its rejection. For in this matter the criticisms against scholasticism are correlatively the defense and proclamation of Teilhard's insight.

The case against post-tridentine scholasticism simmers

15. In what follows I am much indebted to Eulalio R. Baltazar, *Teilhard and the Supernatural,* Baltimore (1966).

16. See e.g., C. Vollert, L. Malvez, A. Brunner, *Theology Digest* 8 (1960), pp. 133-147.

down to this: its theology of the supernatural, characterized
by the twin postulate of two orders (natural and supernatural)
and the phantom state of *pure nature,* is dictated by the exigencies of its own closed, artificial and naturalistic system.
Far from being harmonious with the data of modern science
and of revelation it appears to clash with these.

I *Data of modern science*

The scholastics assume that reality is static; they view
it as a world of *objects,* cut off from and defined against each
other. Given the state of scientific investigation in their age,
their approach was inevitable. The revolution launched by
Galileo and others has invaded every department of knowledge and culture only in the twentieth century. Obviously
Aristotle and the scholastics cannot be blamed for their limitations. Indeed one can only admire the coherence, beauty and
validity of their system within its own rigid structure and
given their premise that the universe is static. Scholasticism
presents a theology cast in the terminology of commonsense
observation. As such it will always retain a relative validity.
Just as commonsense observation cannot be dispensed with
in the affairs of routine living (despite the sophistication
of our technological age, all of us keep referring to sunrises
and sunsets), similarly the scholastic approach enjoys an en-
during prestige. Within its own restricted framework and on
its own premises it represents (in the words of the magisterium) a *philosophia perennis.*

However the modern thinker rightly protests against any
absolutizing and universalizing of this approach, as though
it adequately explained reality as this is manifested to us
today. For reality is not static; it is dynamic and evolutionary.
Hence the scholastic system appears irrelevant to the mass
of non-Christian thinkers, to all Protestant and Greek Ortho-

dox Christians and to the rapidly growing majority of theologians within the Roman communion, who along with the
rest of their contemporaries accept the evolutionary hypothesis.

Modern science transcends the data of the external senses
and demonstrates that we can no longer rely on these with
the naive trust of ancient and medieval man. It convinces us
that we must set aside the limited, even misleading witness
of external sensation and take our stand on evidence sifted
out by the intellect. The table on which I write seems to
my fist and eye solid and stable. In fact I know that it is not
what it seems. It is a field of energy, a gyrating conglomeration
of sub-atomic particles. Hills and valleys, mountains and pre-
cipices seem to be the very incarnation of constancy and
permanence. Indeed within the life-span, not only of a single
individual but even of untold generations of men, their con-
tours have not appreciably altered. But viewed in the actual
perspective of the billions of years of their existence, they
appear, like rivers and streams, ever flowing. Theirs is not
a state of fixed and eternal repose, but of flux and *genesis,* of
historic evolution and unending process. "Whirlpools of energy
dance perpetually to the dizzy rhythm of unceasing rounds."
The molecules of a diamond, symbol of hardness, oscillate
19,000 billion times per second. The iron molecules in a rusty
old screw make 10,000 billion gyrations every second.

Some twentieth century scholastics profess themselves at
ease with these discoveries of modern science. They contend
that evolution, far from destroying scholasticism, actually illustrates its perennial ability to assimilate new data. They
hold that scholasticism's dictum: "no motion without substance or a principle of motion" retains its validity and is
quite simply adjustable to evolution. This they rate as an accidental determination happening to an already given and
self-contained substance—i.e., the universe.

Against this it is urged that scholastic theologians mis-
construe the nature of evolution. An example best illustrates
this point. I lay a seed on a table, turn it around, roll it, subject it to heat and light, flick it backwards and forwards. In
such circumstances, the seed is a subject that perdures and
undergoes various changes; it is a principal and substantial
reality and its different motions are secondary and accidental.
It can thus be satisfactorily described according to the aristotelic categories of substance and accident.

However the picture is transformed when we treat it
truly as a seed, as a carrier of life. Then we plant it in the
soil, we water and cultivate it, give it sunlight and shade,
allow climate to affect it. Now process begins. There is interaction of seed on soil and soil on seed—and other elements
on both. Germination sets in. The seed gives itself to the
soil and in return receives from its environment. It is no longer
an abiding substance affected by various accidental stresses
and motions from without. It is no longer simply a seed in
isolation. It is a seed-in-evolution, a sapling-in-becoming. It
is in process towards tree, blossom, fruit. It is the *alpha*
of a process whose *omega* is the fruit it will eventually produce by way of giving and receiving. Germination cannot be
predicated of the seed in exactly the same manner as were
the passing changes imposed on it while it lay on the table, cut
off from its natural milieu and therefore destined to shrivel
and die. Once lodged in the ground, the seed is no longer
the principal reality. This is rather germination-towards-the-
seedling. Germination is not related to the seed as to a per-
during subject. The seed-in-germination is not a static and
complete essence. Its existence is essentially sharedness, a
towards-the-otherness; it is part of a process; it is a becoming.
Hence, seed, seedling, tree, branch, leaves, flowers are all
to be dynamically referred to the fruit that will emerge as the
term and omega of the process. It is the fruit that endows

the seed with its character and significance. The goal determines the whole process and marks off seed from seed.

Evolution is correctly understood when we look to the analogy not of the seed on the table, but the seed planted in the earth in view of germination and eventual fruit-bearing. Evolution cannot be forced into the mold of substance and accident. The world cannot be separated from the process of evolution as a static substance is divided from its accidents. The universe must not be treated as a complete, self-contained substance undergoing the accidental modification of evolution, or as a source, first established in essential perfection, from which subsequently issues the accidental activity of evolution.

Evolution is, indeed, activity—not accidental nor transient, but immanent. It affects the whole world, but not just as a presupposed substratum, not just as a substance modified by its accidents. The world itself is in dynamic and immanent movement; it was born, it grows and matures. God's creative activity consists in continually endowing the world with more and more dynamic power of self-surpassing and self-realization. The world thus develops and differentiates; it traverses various critical thresholds; after thousands of millions of years of effort it "produces" man. The universe itself is in process, and the proper and adequate subject of attribution when we speak of evolution is the process itself. It is a process of giving and receiving, of dynamic tension and interaction. In such a scheme, existence is not completeness and self-containedness, but sharedness and relatedness. Gathered within the giant process of cosmogenesis are the lesser processes—all with mutual interconnections, and vitally reacting to one another. Every process, whether it be micro- or macro-, is governed by its omega without which no process can have existence or meaning. The orthogenetic evolution of the universe itself is controlled by the Omega of omegas, the Logos incarnate in the world, the lodestar of all processes, the consummation of all reality: Jesus Christ (see Eph 1:23).

The first count against scholasticism is that it attempts to explain the supernatural according to an obsolete pattern of thought, inadequate to account for our actual universe. Its theology is consequently crippled by the defects of its *Weltanschauung*.

II   *Data of revelation*

We offer here A—a general consideration, followed by B—particular elaborations that may serve to elucidate and enforce it.

A: *General consideration*

The most distinctive, original and profound trait of the supernatural as it is revealed in the Scriptures is undoubtedly *personal love*. The revelation of the supernatural pivots around God's initiating, self-communicating, personal love towards men, calling for man's response in love and self-giving, and gathering those beloved into the fellowship (*koinonia*) of the Chosen People.

The scholastic system fails to do justice to the grandeur and amplitude of such a revelation. Its basic structure of substance with the dynamism of act and potency has an individualistic, self-centered, isolationist trend, hostile to essential relatedness.[17] It is therefore charged with (i) borrow-

17. Substance receives acts which perfect it and actualize its potencies. By means of successive actuations it gradually achieves fullness of being, becoming, in the process, more and more autonomous and self-reliant, less and less dependent on others. Act and potency, seeing that they constitute a dynamism not of giving or communication,

ing its notion of love from the individualism of Aristotle; (ii) confusing love with desire, or Christian *agape* with Greek *eros;* (iii) levelling down the Gospel-command to love God above all things to the movement of human desire that coils in on itself; (iv) presenting man's last end not so much as the three-personed God to be loved for his own sake but rather as an *object* whose acquisition, use or fruition is desirable.[18]

This post-tridentine scholastic theology of the supernatural found its reflection in the life of the western Church, especially in the eighteenth and nineteenth centuries: waning of the liturgy; neglect of the doctrine of the Mystical Body; overemphasis on created grace; handling of grace as a sort of supernatural currency; individualistic approach to spirituality, sacraments and indulgences; effort to amass great stores of grace for oneself rather than to promote awareness of others, going out to them in genuine love and service.

The supernatural of revelation seems to sort much better with a teilhardian system whose dynamism is true love, where existence is sharedness and relatedness, where all reality is seen as in a process of becoming and development.

B: *Particular elaborations*

a) *Personality in scholasticism*

Scripture presents the supernatural as pre-eminently personal, as the highest conceivable form of interpersonal com-

---

but of receiving and acquisition, segregate substance from other beings. As the substance gathers into itself more and more perfections, it completes the circle of its isolation from other substances.

---

18. See Baltazar, *op. cit.,* pp. 222-223.

munion between God and man. It is characteristic of scholasticism to de-personalize or "thingify." This is one reason for
its being abandoned by so many today.

Of course the scholastics do not deny personality. On the
contrary, they attribute it to man as a rational animal. However one does not penetrate far in the meaning of personality merely by tabbing a man with the label of personality.
Scholastics are more concerned with man as nature than as
person, with being-as-object, rather than with being-as-sub-
ject. They investigate personality only in so far as it can be
"thingified" or transformed into an object. They approach
man in much the same manner as they approach a stock or
a stone: something knowable as object. To know a person
in terms of his nature is to know him only as a *thing*. It is
not to know him as a unique and ineffable *I* or *Thou* seizable
only in direct encounter or through mutual love. The scholastic thus halts at man's objective surface, the sum of deter-
minations by which he is conceptually defined. He fails to
reach to a man's depth as a unique subsistent, a self-revealing
plenitude, a peerless center and source of free initiative and
love. The person, reduced to a supposit ticketed rational, is
viewed from the outside, is conceptualized and objectivized.
His originality as a subject, the abyss of his selfhood, his core,
his inner life are pushed aside as peripheral, accidental, irrelevant. In the necessary and universal world that scholasticism studies, the *I*, being ephemeral and contingent, appears
as a blemish, an anomaly and a diminishment.[19]

To people struck by Teilhard's vision, scholasticism seems
a sorry sort of vehicle for conveying the grandeur of the
supernatural. Worse still, it seems actually to block the appreciation of the supernatural as a loving, personal, *I-Thou*
dialogue between the triune God and man.

19. Cf. R. Johann quoted by Baltazar, *op. cit.*, pp. 216-229.

b) *Immanence of the supernatural*

Any satisfactory theology of the supernatural must hold in balanced tension both its transcendence and its immanence. Can scholasticism pass muster here? To answer this question we must pause a moment over the salient feature of post-tridentine scholasticism: namely, its two-order system (with which, of course, is connected its invention of the state of pure nature: theorizing about this, one can discern what is owed and what is gratuitous to human nature).

For the scholastic, reality is a static and two-staged edifice: the natural groundfloor of the creator-God and the supernatural, upper storey of the redeemer-Christ.

The first order is wholly natural. It is presented as complete, self-enclosed and autonomous. By definition, it is equipped with its own laws, principles, properties and commensurate end. It is neither redemptive nor supernatural but purely neutral. In it God functions exclusively as creator, conservator and ruler. It has no structuring towards the incarnation. Apart altogether from Christ, it enjoys its all-rounded intelligibility and *raison d'être*. It is cosmology pure and simple without any admixture of soteriology.

The second is the supernatural order. It comes from above and from without to a previously fully constituted cosmos. The supernatural thus appears somewhat like icing on a cake or a veneer on furniture. It affords the facilities within which salvation-history can unfold. It is detachable from the meaning and the existence of man and his world. Like the natural order, the supernatural too has its own end (new and transcendent) together with all the required and proportionate means to attain the same. The scholastic system thus postulates *in theory* two ends for man though it recognizes *in practice* that he is destined exclusively to a supernatural consummation.

This twofold system is one of the main buttresses upholding the scholastic position on the transcendence of the supernatural. We must return to this paramount point in sections
c), d) and e) *infra*. What we wish to stress at the moment is
that transcendence is only half of the dogma of the supernatural. For, besides this, revelation equally strongly underscores the immanence of the supernatural or man's need of
it, his yearning and unquenchable thirst for it (cf. the caden-
ced phrase of the collect, first Tuesday of Lent: . . . *praesta ut
apud te mens nostra tuo desiderio fulgeat . . .*). It is this
aspect that is passionately voiced by the psalmist (e.g., Ps 42
& Ps 73, 23-28) and cast in imperishable language by Augustine: "You have made us for yourself, Lord, and restless is
our heart until it rests in You" (*Conf.* I.I). This immanent or
intrinsic quality is vividly translated into practice by the
holiest Christians who conduct their lives in the intimate
awareness of their need of Christ. They know that without
him they can do nothing; they acknowledge him as the way,
the truth, the light and the life; that, indeed, he is all and
in all (Col 3:11). Incidentally the immanence of the supernatural is emphatic in St. Thomas, whose thinking (we remind ourselves once more) is *not* identical with that of the
post-tridentine scholastics.[20]

The scholastic two-world theory hardly safeguards the immanence of the supernatural. It cannot lend itself to convincing men that they should strive after such a supernatural.
Stripped of all intrinsic orientation to the supernatural, man
(as the scholastics present him) is reduced to an integral
part of a wholly self-sufficient system. Why, then, should he
bestir and sacrifice himself for what in last analysis is classed
as an accidental perfection, a juxtaposed adornment, a non-
essential increment, an invasion of his cosy little world from

20. See Max Seckler, *Instinkt und Glaubenswille* (1961), p. 144.

some infinitely remote and quite foreign sphere? If, as the scholastics teach him, man really does belong to a solidly determined and substantially complete world of his own, he may be pardoned his lukewarmness at the prospect of a supernatural which, far from answering any pressing and profound need of his being, can appear to him only as an adventitious luxury or a capricious embellishment.

The scholastic device of two orders, each with its commensurate end, seems to modern theologians to betray a quite superficial, even a cavalier attitude to the final end of a personal creature. In a quite offhand fashion, one can assign a *thing* various ends. One may use one's alarm-clock as a time-piece, an ornament, a book-end, a paperweight or as a prop to keep the door ajar. But the last end of a person cannot be switched and changed with such insouciance. A person is structured on and exists to attain his end. He can be understood only in view of his end; he is definable only by taking his end into cognizance.

It must be stressed that the idea of man as a creature of two ends can claim the patronage almost only of the post-tridentine scholastics. It has no basis in the Scriptures or in patristic tradition. It is completely foreign to the thinking not only of St. Augustine but also of St. Thomas. The following words of this latter would faithfully mirror the mind of all except the post-tridentine theologians:

Quamvis enim homo naturaliter inclinetur in finem ultimum, non tamen potest naturaliter illum consequi, sed solum per gratiam, et hoc est propter eminentiam illius finis.[21]

For man, though naturally orientated towards his last end, cannot reach it by the resources of nature, but only by grace—and this because of the transcendence of that end.

21. *In Boeth., De Trin.*, 6.4 ad 5. On the meaning of *naturaliter* here

According to perhaps the unanimity of non-scholastic Christian thinkers, man is intrinsically ordained to the supernatural which however he will actually seize only with the help of elevating grace.

c) *Transcendence of the supernatural: man*

Why do post-tridentine scholastics reduce the supernatural to an outside and adventitious element? The answer is plain: their solicitude to protect the transcendence or gratuity of the supernatural. If, they urge, the supernatural is immanent, intrinsic and needed by nature, it ceases to be gratuitous. For gratuity is shielded only when there is absence of claim, of exigency or of necessity. If a man is intrinsically ordained to the supernatural, he can demand it and so it ceases to be gratuitous. If no longer gratuitous, it is no longer transcendent nor supernatural.

We must remind ourselves of the framework within which scholastics operate. It is a framework of natures, not of persons, of juridic relationships, not of love and interpersonal communion. Within such a framework intrinsic ordination does assuredly spell exigence; and this in its turn undermines first the gratuity and eventually the very supernaturality of the supernatural.

The teilhardian thinker lodges his protest not against the logic (which is flawless) but against the premise or system of the scholastics. Taking his stand on the Scriptures, he

see M. Seckler, *op. cit.,* pp. 133-136. E. Schillebeeckx describes as "pure historical Thomism" this statement: Man's being is such that the beatific vision is *natural* to him even though it transcends his power and is therefore *supernatural*. (*Concept of Truth and Theological Renewal,* London, 1968, p. 47).

denies that the supernatural can be satisfactorily expounded in terms of natures whose interconnections must indeed be expressed in the juridical language of rights, duties and exigencies. He maintains that the supernatural is explainable not in the vocabulary of justice but of charity.[22]

To equate personal encounter with contractual justice can only mislead. A gardener, for example, works under contract for a certain wage. When he has industriously finished his job, in sheer justice he can lay claim to payment. But it would be a crazy disproportion for him to demand as his reward the hand of the employer's daughter. Marriage swings around authentic love and interpersonal communion. It cannot be whittled down to an impersonal legal contract (even though it has, of course, its contractual side).

The supernatural likewise belongs first and foremost to the field of personal dialogue and friendship where the spontaneity and gratuitousness of chivalrous love dominate. In true love, the *I* needs the *thou* and can find and integrate himself only in self-gift to a *thou*. But although the *I* is structured on the *thou*, union with the *thou* is always gratuitous because it is (*ex hypothesi*) a union of true, personal love which cannot not be free. As Teilhard says: "to say *love* is to say *liberty*" (*The Future of Man*, 1969, p. 140). Juridical claims and exactions make no sense in the realm of personal communion. Only through love can *I* attain, but never coerce, a *thou*. If another person gives himself it is always out of the sovereign freedom of love. By definition, finite personality is not self-sufficient. I need other persons in order to discover myself. Yet another person's self-gift in love is beyond my

---

22. One might apply here St. Bernard's words: *Affectus est, non contractus: nec acquiritur pacto, nec acquirit. Sponte afficit, et spontaneum facit* (De diligendo Deo, 7.17, *Opera* (1963), 3, pp. 133-134.

claims and my powers of coercion. Interpersonal communion is always and mutually gratuitous.

So with the supernatural friendship between man and God. The fact of man's structuring and orientation to the supernatural gives man no exigency for it. In no wise does it destroy the gratuity of the supernatural. By definition this belongs to the field of personal love and so is beyond the reach of law and exigency (cf. Gal 5:18: "If you are led by the Spirit, no law can touch you . . ."). God alone can initiate it and he does so gratuitously and only gratuitously.

We need to go further. Intrinsic ordination to the supernatural, far from threatening its gratuity and transcendence, is in fact the climate required in order that gratuity should flourish. Why cannot a man enter into a personal friendship with a rose-bush or a canary? Because he is not intrinsically structured to these objects. His structuring is reserved to persons. On the contrary, marriage is so eminent an example of interpersonal communion because man and woman are physically, physiologically, emotionally and mentally ordained to one another. Nevertheless their mutual intrinsic ordination in no way menaces the gratuity of their reciprocal love.

The supernatural concerns man's meeting with the self-communicating God. From the very roots of his being he is structured and orientated to this loving God (*intimior intimo meo*—as Augustine puts it; "not far from any one of us"—as Paul says: Acts 17:27). When God comes to man in the free initiative of his love, man, because of his ordination to God, is able to abandon himself with all the strength of his being to this almighty Lover, source of man's existence, its goal and intelligibility. It is man's intrinsic structuring to the self-communicating God, whom he needs more than anything else, that conditions the feasibility of this sovereignly gratuitous and most lofty interpersonal communion.

d) *Transcendence of the supernatural: the universe*

Here we canvass once more the same questions as in c) above—with, however, a shift in emphasis. The center of interest is no longer *man* but his *universe* and its relation to the supernatural.[23] How stands the world towards Christ? Can one maintain that the universe is geared on the incarnation? Is the incarnate Word the target and lodestar of evolution? Is Christ intrinsic or extrinsic to creation? Is cosmogenesis essentially Christogenesis? In short—is there a total and finished natural as well as supernatural order?

The scholastic position is sharp-etched—as was explained in (b) *supra*. Once again the reason commanding it is eagerness to defend the transcendence or gratuity of the supernatural. On scholastic premises, to admit a world intrinsically structured on the incarnation is tantamount to denying the supernatural. For the scholastic, intrinsic ordination spells exigency which, in its turn, destroys gratuity. To eschew this disastrous consequence, he can see only one escape: to postulate a twin, "bicephalic" universe.

Teilhardian theology finds the scholastic position unsatisfactory on more than one count. First, it undermines the dignity and rôle of Christ; it leads to an enfeebled christology. Christ comes to a world that is complete, intelligible and self-contained; it has no essential need of him, no structuring towards him. It can hardly be called in the full sense *his own* (cf. Jn 1:11). Hence he comes from outside, as a stranger, even as an intruder. He is an epiphenomenon, a desirable but superfluous ornament set on a closed, intrinsically perfect order. The incarnation is reduced to an accident of history. It is imposed on the world from on

23. See Baltazar, *op. cit.*, pp. 265-306.

high by a divine declarative decision. The cosmic dimension
that Sts. John and Paul assign to Christ are interpreted not
in a physical or ontological, but in a juridical sense.[24]

Next, the modern theologian here as elsewhere objects
to the methodology of scholasticism on the ground that it
does not permit of a free and frank enquiry into the meaning
of revelation. It implies on the contrary a cutting down of
revelation to the measure of its system. The scholastics do
not first and foremost consult sacred Scripture, impartially
and scientifically assessing its witness and only then taking
up position, gradually elaborating their theology of the supernatural. Their procedure is diametrically opposed. They start
with their system and interrogate Scripture only in the second
instance. Its witness is forced into the mold of their system.

In the matter before us, the question to be answered is
this: does Scripture endorse the two-order universe of the
scholastics? The answer must be negative. Scripture, whether
of the OT or of the NT, gives no hint of two, distinct divine
acts resulting in two separate orders, one exclusively natural
and cosmological and the other exclusively supernatural and
soteriological. Quite the reverse. The OT consistently presents
a covenanted universe, where creation is simply the first
in a long series of Yahweh's saving acts in favor of his
people.[25] These salvific interventions culminate in the NT
with Christ—in his incarnation, passion, death, resurrection
and ascension. The NT Christology of John (see e.g., prologue)
and of Paul (see e.g., Colossians) forbids any dichotomy between a God-line of creation and a Christ-line of redemption.
And just as in the OT man and his world are intelligible only

24. See discussion by C. F. Mooney, *Theol. Studies* 25 (1964), pp.
576-610.
25. See e.g., Est 4:17a-17i; Is 42:5-16; 43:1; Ps 77 (76):17-21; 145
(144):13-18; cf. St. John Chrysostom, *In Jn. hom.*, 14, PG 59.94.

in the perspective of the Covenant, so in the NT: all being and all intelligibility are in function of Christ. He is the light of the world, a light which is life (Jn 8:12; 9:5); in fact, *the* way, *the* truth, *the* life (Jn 14:6). Without him man cannot so much as lift his finger (Jn 15:5).

The scholastic, if he is to meet the demands of his dualistic system, has to whittle away the force and boldness of these scriptural statements. Teilhard and modern theologians, on the contrary, prefer to start with them and accept them at their face value. Consequently they admit only one order and that salvific. They see the whole of reality in a slow march towards Christ, the omega point, principle of universal vitality. They see everything in the world and the world itself simply as an expression of the Father's gratuitous love and of his decree to deify man and exalt reality in and through Christ who "invests himself organically with the very majesty of his creation" (*The Phenomenon of Man,* p. 325). There are not two separate orders; there is just one evolving universe which is penetrated at its creation and at every subsequent phase of its growth by the same loving salvific care of the Father of mercies in Christ.[26]

Of course creation is not salvific in exactly the same sense and to the same degree as is e.g., the passion of Christ. The universe evolves and crosses various critical thresholds, releasing new dimensions of being. Salvation likewise unfolds its history and has its phases of ripening development. The salvific process is directed to Christ and his *pleroma,* and to the beatific vision as the consummation for the individual. Things may be more or less salvific according to the closeness or relative looseness of their connection with Christ.

26. "Il ne saurait pas plus y avoir deux sommets au Monde que deux centres à une corconférence" (Teilhard, *Hymne de l'univers,* 1961, p. 238).

An illustration may help. So far as fruitfulness is concerned, there is a marked difference between a stone and a seed. The sown seed, though at present far removed from bearing fruit, is nevertheless in process towards sapling, tree, blossom and fruit. It may, therefore, be termed fruitful even now in a way not applicable to the stone. So it is with creation. Obviously it is not salvific as is the resurrection, nor supernatural as is adoptive sonship. Yet in so far as its whole *raison d'être* is to manifest God's gratuitous love of man, and to inaugurate a giant organic movement climaxing in incarnation and beatific vision, it may be described as salvific and supernatural. The affirmation that the order of creation is in fact salvific and supernatural, is tantamount to affirming that it is Christ's order; he belongs to it and it to him. He is the lodestar and the fruit of evolution. He does not come to a strange and foreign country, self-contained and complete; he comes to his own.

But does not such a notion imply that the universe is able to produce Christ from its own resources? So it appears to all mesmerized by scholastic postulates. The difficulty vanishes for those who frankly accept a dynamic, evolutionary universe. Evolution means that a "less" is transformed into a "more," and therefore that the essential being of the world surpasses itself. This in its turn demands the Absolute who from outside the world enables new forces to enter the world.[27] The very hypothesis of a world in process to Christ-Omega involves the self-*in*sufficiency of this world. An evolving world cannot dictate to God, or educe him from its own potentialities; it can only appeal to him as its supreme *other*. It needs him and is structured on him; it is too stricken with creaturely poverty ever to be able to claim or produce him.

27. Cf. L. Boros, *Concilium* 10 (1970), pp. 15-16.

Just as the seed or the human person can develop and achieve fulfillment only through an exchange of giving and receiving with an other, so with the world. It must receive from God and vitally respond to him.

As we have already admitted, in a scholastic dualistic framework studded with natures and juridic entities, intrinsic ordination means exigency. In the *de facto* reality of a single evolving universe lapped around by God's gratuitous love, intrinsic ordination does not undermine gratuity. It enhances it. Everything in the present dispensation hangs on the Father's personal love. Every part is gratuitous with the gratuity of the whole. The universe is a tight organic unity shaped by the saving mercy of the Father in Christ. Difficulties arise when we allow our minds to fragment and dissect this unity. While we keep it in perspective all goes well. From all eternity the Father has *freely* decreed Christ as Savior and Center of the universe. All individual phases, parts and intrinsic structuring are caught up under the overriding gratuity of God's total aim. The internal ordering of particular segments to the incarnation does not *coerce* God nor rob him of his freedom. It is his own spontaneous decree to communicate himself in Christ that commands the structuring of every portion and of the whole process. Were God compelled by some *outside* authority to give Christ, his freedom would be shackled. Of course nothing of the sort happens. Nothing foreign to God coerces him. It is his own bounteous initiative that determines him to orientate the world and all in it intrinsically to Christ-Omega.

e) *Witness of Scripture*

This section contains nothing new. Its scope is to hammer home the points already made about the data of revelation by gathering them together in an express appeal to Scripture and by pondering in particular the capital theme of the Covenant.[28] The OT is concerned immediately with the Chosen People. This People is, however, a type embodying all humanity. Hence what the OT teaches is, *mutatis mutandis,* "true not only for Israel as a people but for each Israelite; and because Israel is a type of all humanity, what is true for Israel is true for all humanity collectively and singly. The historical events that happened to Israel in the nation's relation with Yahweh are recapitulated in the spiritual life of every Christian." [29]

The covenant-theme teaches i) that man is intrinsically ordained to the covenanting God; ii) that he is inextricably bound up with God so that he cannot exist, think or work in isolation; iii) that his very being is towards that supreme Other; iv) that apart from the Covenant he is insubstantial and unthinkable.

Moreover man's relationship to God is defined as inter-personal communion based on love. This notion is conveyed by the prolongation of the covenant-theme in the direction of marriage (e.g., Ho 2:4-25; Is 54:5; 61:10; 62:1-5; Jr 2: 2; 3:20; 31:32; Ep 5:22-33). To seize the full force of the lesson inculcated under this imagery, one needs to recall the Hebrew view on sex and marriage—widely divergent from the more familiar scholastic approach.

As we have seen, the scholastics objectivized and deper-sonalized everything they studied. They were interested in universals, in natures, not in persons. Consistently with their system, they "thingified" sex, labelling it *accident.* Inevitably,

28. See Baltazar, *op. cit.,* pp. 246-264.
29. *Ibid.,* p. 249. See the *Exsultet* of the Easter Vigil. Also the prayer after the third reading: "May the peoples of the world become true sons of Abraham and prove worthy of the heritage of Israel."

then, they were led to treat it superficially.

For the Hebrews, on the contrary, sex was anything but superficial. They regarded it as constitutive of men and women as persons. In their view, each sex is made for the other. Woman is intrinsically ordained to man and structured on him —and *vice versa*. From this essential structuring results marriage—primary form of interpersonal communion. Forcefully Scripture describes this profound and intimate union as man and woman becoming one flesh (Gn 2:34; Mt 19:5; I Cor 6: 16; Ep 5:31). It assigns to wedded love a pre-eminence outmatching even the affection binding parents and children (Gn 2:22-24). For the Hebrews, therefore, feminine-masculine polarity touches human existence at its very core.

It is against this background of sex in the semitic culture that we must assess the relationship between man and God conveyed by the Bible under the symbol of the Covenant. Man's ordination to God cannot, therefore, be whittled away to something purely accidental and extrinsic. According to the deepest center in him, he is structured on the all-loving God— much as woman is structured on man.

In order to elucidate man's supernatural union with God, St. Paul borrowed the OT covenant-theme in its marriage dress (Ep 5:21-33). But with St. Paul everything is drawn into sharper focus and made more concrete. His concern is no longer immediately God and men at large, not even Yahweh and the Chosen People; it is narrowed down directly to Christ and Christians. Sex itself is caught up in the baptismal consecration to, and solidarity with Christ. Hence when Christians marry, their union at once becomes a symbol of Christ's union with his august bride, the Church. St. Paul further enforces the intimacy of the union between Christ and Christians by his allegory of head and body. St. John's parallel is vine and branches. Without the head/vine the body/branches are nothing and can effect nothing. Both Paul and John thus suggest an intrinsic ordination of Christians to Christ, a structuring on him at least as intimate as woman's on man.

If, however, Scripture is emphatic about man's intrinsic ordination to God, it proclaims with equal emphasis that this does not entitle man to any *claim* on God and his love. It is Yahweh who initiates the Covenant and issues the invitation to his partner. With untrammelled freedom, he communicates himself. He chooses whom he wills. Nothing could be plainer and more explicit than this theme which runs up and down the length and breadth of OT and NT (e.g., it is implied or expressed with every mention of the Covenant. Consider the force of Gn 15; see also Ez 16:1-14; Ho 2; Rm 9:10-18; Jn 6:44; 15:16). The individual's supernatural union with God and possession of him, the world's slow progress towards Christ, its Omega—these are beyond the grasp of unaided created resources. The creature may be intrinsically orientated to the Father of mercies giving himself to individuals and to the world in Christ, but God comes of his own free volition, not at man's bidding. He is the transcendent God infinitely beyond the created universe, which, however, he has structured towards him. When, then, he stoops to communicate himself in Christ he comes to what is his own and to what needs him. It is so much his own that without his descent in Christ it has no final intelligibility or existence. It is so wholly geared on Christ that if Christ is taken away it is non-sense, non-being. So it is with every process: remove the *other*, cut out the dynamism of love and there remains only dismantling, disintegration and death. The message of Scripture is that the supernatural is not only gratuitous and transcendent; it is likewise and somehow immanent and intrinsic. Like Scripture, a theology of the supernatural is bound to include both elements in the dogma of the supernatural and to hold them in balanced tension; it must extract from their dialectical encounter the complexity of revealed truth.

It is argued here that Teilhard achieves this, whereas scholasticism sadly fails.[30]

PART III: *Evaluation*

Scholastic not necessarily aristotelic and thomist

In assessing the charges levelled by Dr. Baltazar at the scholastic theory of the supernatural we need carefully to distinguish the positions defended by the post-tridentine scholastics from the genuine thought of Aristotle and of St. Thomas. An injustice could be done to both these geniuses were one to assume that everything commonly labelled aristotelic, thomist or scholastic faithfully mirrored their views or was the legitimate prolongation of their principles.

Whatever the merits of Dr. Baltazar's criticisms of scholasticism as a static, self-centered system, they appear wide of the mark when referred to *Aristotle's* dynamic presentation of nature's intrinsically and endlessly becoming, substantially changing and in movement under the drive of environment and under the magnetism of what was for him the dominating factor, i.e., the end. It would not perhaps be fanciful to suggest that Teilhard's omega of cosmic evolution, far from being the antithesis of Aristotle's *telos* or Prime Mover is in fact its embellishment and transfiguration. To explain an

30. The same case in favor of man's being intrinsically structured on God can be strongly urged from, and is corroborated by the Hebrew concept of Yahweh, Lord and Giver of *life*. The semitic concept of the life that God gives is extremely dense and rich. It includes, besides bare existence, might, solidity, security, health, blessing, joy, salvation AND particularly the gift of God's self in love and friendship. See G. Greshake, *Auferstehung der Toren*, Essen (1969), pp. **175-185.**

evolving universe there is more in Aristotle's metaphysics than is commonly conceded today. He lacked what was, by the nature of the case, beyond his reach: the equipment of modern science and the data of Christian revelation.

Further, outstanding modern scholars recognize about St. *Thomas*—(i) that he taught man's intrinsic but gratuitous ordination to the beatific vision, while at the same time unequivocally holding that it was attainable only by grace; (ii) that he knew nothing of the later *Deus-ex-machina* theory of pure nature with its concomitant dualism of orders;[31] (iii) that, therefore, he did not conceive of nature in so static a fashion as the post-tridentine scholastics.

Substantial change

Perhaps the criticisms of Dr. Baltazar do not sufficiently allow for the fact that the scholastics admitted, beyond accidental, also substantial change. Their principles do not preclude the crossing of a critical threshold, even the possibility of life in a test-tube. So perhaps they can account for process and true evolution not only of individual things but even of the universe.

Out-of-favor scholasticism not devoid of value

The onslaughts of modern theology against scholasticism

31. M. Seckler well says: "Thomas kennt zwar ein doppeltes Ziel des Menschen: ein natürliches und ein ubernatürliches; das der Philosophen und das der Theologen; *beatitudo perfecta* and *beatitudo imperfecta.* Aber er kennt kein natürliches Endziel *ausserhalb* der Erde—auch nicht hypothetischerweise. Wo immer er von einem natürlichen Endziel spricht, versteht er es als rein irdisches Glück ... Aber er sieht darin keine definitive Alternative" (*Instinkt und Glaubenswille,* pp. 203-204).

cannot be lightly dismissed. Apart altogether from the question of their intrinsic merit there is the objective, incontestable fact that everywhere within the Church itself scholasticism is slipping more and more into disfavor. Fewer and fewer mature thinkers have any confidence in its relevancy today while the younger men are, as a body, not only disinterested in it as a system but often quite hotly hostile. The ranks of its critics are forever swelling while the ranks of its friends keep dwindling.

Two editions of H. de Lubac's *Surnaturel* symbolize the rapid change in climate. This important work repudiates the dualism of post-tridentine scholasticism. When it first appeared in 1946, it became a center of controversy and was looked on askance. Its re-editing in two volumes in 1965 is serenely and respectfully saluted by the majority of theologians who appear to take its main thesis for granted.[32] Teilhard de Chardin is still something of a stormy-petrel. He continues to be rebuked for vagueness or (what is grossly unfair) even for pantheism. This or that argument is mauled; this or that lacuna underlined. Nevertheless one grows accustomed to hearing references to *the era of Teilhard,* to the impossibility of putting back the clock, to the fact that his basic insights are acquired.

Certain values in the scholastic approach must not be lost sight of. In this age of phenomenal, technical advance in photography, one normally prefers (for the sake of verisimilitude) motion pictures to stills. However, if one wishes to watch closely the movements of (say) a hurdler, slow motion shots and stills are indispensable. Likewise in the field of theology. Plainly the existential and personalist approach is more relevant to modern man and better adapted

32. See e.g., *Down Rev* 85 (1966), pp. 397-407. Cf. however, C. Boyer, *Greg* 28 (1947), pp. 379-395 and 58 (1967), pp. 130-132.

to conveying the scriptural message. However, for a more complete probing of truth, objectivizing and analyzing remain indispensable. The pitfall to be shunned is a twin exclusivism. The exclusivism of the modern who is so attached to the categories of intersubjectivity and encounter that he entirely overlooks the *ontological* implications of our supernatural communion with God. The exclusivism of the scholastic who flatters himself that his abstractive, conceptualizing metaphysics furnish the *only* orthodox theology of the supernatural. We must not erect any human construct into an idol, nor may we imagine that the infinite riches of revelation can be *adequately* channelled through any single human formula.

As regards the transcendence and gratuity of the supernatural: we must acknowledge the correctness of the scholastic position (in particular that intrinsic ordination means exigency) *if* we concede its premises: a static universe; a limited time-scale; a philosophy of natures with their juridically conceived interrelations; an order of creation completely independent of the order of redemption. If however we accept the findings of modern science about a dynamic universe evolving across millions of years, if we take the scriptural pre-eminence assigned to Christ literally and ontologically, not just metaphorically and juridically, we will not necessarily jeopardize gratuity simply because we view man and his world as inwardly ordered towards the supernatural. Modern research would seem to suggest that at this point the critics of post-tridentine scholasticism are much closer to Augustine and Thomas than are their victims.[33]

However we can concur with the opinion of E. Schillebeeckx, O.P.: it is not the aristotelic concept of human nature that forces us, as believers, to some sort of distinction between

33. See e.g., M. Seckler, *op. cit.*, pp. 140-143; 171-220.

nature and the supernatural. Rather it is the very essence
of grace as God's spontaneous gift of himself. This presupposes the concept of an "ungraced" man, able freely to
welcome or to rebuff God's self-communication. Consequently
nature and the supernatural must be distinguished. But at the
same time their existential unity must be proclaimed.[34]

Kerygmatic theology

The post-Vatican Church is insisting on a theology that
is scripturally, liturgically, pastorally and ecumenically orientated. The modern student knows from history as well as
from personal experience that scholasticism is bereft of this
quartet of qualities, which indeed seem precluded by its
congenital, aprioristic rigidity. For this reason he cannot be
blamed for the dislike he manifests towards scholasticism.

On the other hand, it is assuredly excessive to repudiate
(as some certainly do) all manipulation of metaphysics in the
study of Christianity or every form of conceptualized, scientific theology on the ground that it possesses no pastoral value
whatsoever. The preacher who is trained in systematic theology (provided of course that he understands men in their
concrete situation) has a notable advantage over a colleague
who has scornfully neglected accurate investigation and definition of the content of faith. For the more penetrating insight into the mysteries of faith possessed by the former enables him, within the limits of orthodoxy, to deal easily, vari-
ously and fruitfully with dogmas in a fashion quite beyond
the reach of the latter. It seems unlikely that we shall hear
worthwhile dogmatic homilies from a preacher who has never

34. See "Theologia or Oikonomia," *Concept of Truth and Theological Renewal,* London (1968), p. 89; also pp. 79-105 and 106-154.

embarked on a close scrutiny and serious analysis of the revealed truths.[35]

Exigencies of new knowledge

"It is unwise to pour new wine into old skins." Perhaps this old adage epitomizes the uneasiness of many modern theologians vis-à-vis scholasticism. Echoing Vatican II, they confidently affirm that beneath all changes there are many things which do not change because they have their last foundation in Christ who is the same yesterday, today and forever (*Gaudium et spes*, 10). They have no hesitation in proclaiming the permanence and immutability of Christ and the things necessarily connected with Christ. But they raise the query: "is scholastic metaphysics one of these absolutely indefectible elements?" They are, of course, prepared to admit (as was urged in part II) that the concept of a *philosophia perennis* has a validity, and that the scholastic system is such within its assumptions of (i) a limited time scheme (ii) a static universe (iii) commonsense observation (iv) ordinary language (sunrises, sunsets). But they wonder whether any man-made metaphysics can have the absoluteness and universality that we attribute to Christ. They must not be misunderstood. They are not insinuating that one must change one's metaphysics with every fresh discovery published by research scientists. They do not deny that metaphysics has a certain transcendence over physical science. But (they ask) must one maintain the absoluteness of a metaphysics even when the basic assumptions on which it is constructed are shattered? We now know (i) the quasi-infinity of our space-time con-

---

35. See Schillebeeckx, *op. cit.*, pp. 101-102. See also the observations of K. Rahner: "La situation actuelle de la théologie en Allemagne," published in *Islam—civilisation et religion*, Paris, (1965), pp. 209-227.

tinuum, (ii) that the universe is ever evolving, (iii) that commonsense observation must yield place to intellectual evidence, (iv) that ordinary language does not convey a correct picture of reality.

Besides, we have a different concept of history from that of ancient and medieval man, and our outlook is wholly future-oriented. We face reality not so much to contemplate as to shape it. We are conscious that here and now we are building the future.[36]

May one not suspect the suitability of the scholastic system to cope with our new information? It philosophizes about static *essences* and *beings*. The modern theologian needs, as his instrument, a philosophy of process concerned with *becoming* and *genesis*. This is what Dr. Baltazar has commendably attempted to offer him, thus systematizing the insights of Teilhard de Chardin.

A final word. The modern Christian regards scholasticism as abstract, sterile, divorced from reality. He dislikes its cavalier brushing aside of history, the scant attention it pays to the lessons, facts and unfolding processes of history. He has become keenly alerted to the historical dimension and has recognized a fourth dimension: time. He sees development as an inner dynamic of man's existence whether on the individual, communitarian or cosmic level. He feels an affinity for the post-Vatican II theologians because of their fresh appreciation of the *gesta Dei*: the mighty deeds of the Lord of history on behalf of his people and his interventions in salvation-history. These *gesta Dei* form for the modern Christian the first object of theological enquiry which is indeed much more historical than metaphysical. It is not the "new and the modern" approaches which disconcert him but rather

36. See the pertinent observations of J. B. Metz, *Theology of the World*, New York (1960), especially pp. 80-100.

those of the scholastics with their sorry lack of historical perspective and their static, "atomized" view of human nature.
For he realizes that the so-called new and modern is not only,
naturally, more appealing to him but also actually older,
more authentic and closer to the revealed message. Hence his
delight in the rediscovery in present day theology of the rich
and inspiring tradition of the NT, of the Liturgy and of the
patristic writers.

SELECT BIBLIOGRAPHY

Alfaro, J.,
i) "Natur und Gnade," ii) "Natura pura" *Lexikon für Theologie und Kirche* (1962), 7, pp. 830-835, 809-810; iii) "The supernatural: immanent and transcendent" *Theology Digest,* 8 (1960), pp. 30-34.

Alszeghy, Z.,
"La teologia dell'ordine soprannaturale nella scolastica antica," *Gregorianum* 31 (1950), pp. 414-450.

Aubert, R.,
Le problème de l'acte de foi, Louvain (1950).

Auer, J.,
"Der Begriff des 'Ubernatürlichen' " *Die Entwicklung der Gnadenlehre in der Hochscholastik,* 2, Freiburg (1951).

Bainvel, J. V.,
Nature et surnaturel, Paris (1911).

Baltazar, E. R.,
Teilhard and the Supernatural, Baltimore (1966).

von Balthasar, H. U.,
"Der Begriff der Natur in der Theologie" *Zeitschrift für katholische Theologie,* 75 (1955), pp. 452-461.

Baumgartner, Ch.,
Le mystère chrétien — La grâce du Christ, Tournai (1963).

Beumer, J.,
"Das Verhältnis von geschaffener und ungeschaffener Gnade" *Wissenschaft und Weisheit* (1943), pp. 22-42.

Billot, L.,
De gratia Christi, Rome (1928).

de Broglie, G.,
i) *De fino ultimo humanae vitae,* Paris (1948).
ii) "De la place du surnaturel dans la philosophie de s. Thomas," *Recherches de science religieuse* 14 (1924), pp. 193-246.

de Broglie, P.,
Le surnaturel, Paris (1905).

THE SUPERNATURAL

Bouillard, H.,
  i) "L'intention fondamentale de M. Blondel et la théologie," *Rech. de science religieuse* 36 (1949), pp. 321-402.
  ii) *Blondel et le christianisme*, Paris (1961).
  iii) *Conversion et grâce chez s. Thomas d'Aquin*, Paris (1944).
  iv) "L'Idée de surnaturel et le mystère chrétien," *L'homme devant Dieu*, Paris (1964) 3, pp. 153-166.
Boyer, C.,
  "Nature pure et surnaturel dans le *Surnaturel* du Père de Lubac," *Gregorianum* 28 (1947), pp. 379-395.
Brisbois, E.,
  "Le désir de voir Dieu et la métaphysique du vouloir selon saint Thomas," *Nouvelle revue théologique* 63 (1936), pp. 978-989, 1089-1113.
Burrell, D.,
  "Indwelling: Presence and Dialogue," *Theological Studies* 22 (1961), pp. 1-17.
Colombo, G.,
  "Il problema del soprannaturale negli ultimi cinquant'anni," *Problemi e orientamenti de teologia dommatica*, Milan (1957) 2, pp. 545-607.
Cooke, B. J.,
  Christian Sacraments and Christian Personality, New York (1965), pp. 1-69.
Cuskelly, E. J.,
  The Kindness of God, Cork (1967).
De Letter, P.,
  "Grace, Incorporation, Inhabitation," *Theological Studies* 19 (1958), pp. 1-31.
Deneffe, A.,
  "Geschichte des Wortes 'supernaturalis,'" *Zeitschrift für kath. Theologie* 46 (1922), pp. 337-360.
Donnelly, M.,
  i) "The theory of R. P. M. de la Taille on the Hypostatic Union," *TheolStudies* 2 (1941), pp. 510-526.
  ii) "The Inhabitation of the Holy Spirit...," *TheolStudies* 8 (1947), pp. 445-471.
Donnelly, P., "A recent critique of P. de Lubac's *surnaturel*," *TheolStudies* 9 (1948), pp. 554-561.

Dockx, S.,
   Fils de Dieu par grâce, Paris (1948).
Dumont, P.,
   "La caractère divin de la grâce d'après la théologie scholastique,"
   Revue des sciences religieuses 14 (1935), p. 94.
Flick, M., Alszeghy, Z.,
   "L'opzione fondamentale della vita morale e la grazia," *Gregorianum*
   41 (1960), pp. 593-619.
Fortman, E. J.,
   The Theology of Man and Grace: Commentary, Milwaukee (1966).
Fransen, P.,
   i) *The New Life of Grace*, London (1969).
   ii) "How can non-Christians find salvation?" *Christian Revelation
   and World Religions*, ed. J. Neuner, London (1967), pp. 67-122.
Galtier, P.,
   De ss. Trinitate in se et in nobis, Paris (1933).
Gleason, R. W.,
   The Indwelling Spirit, New York (1966).
González, S., Sagüés, J.,
   "De gratia," *Sacrae Theologiae Summa*, BAC, Madrid (1961) 3,
   pp. 483-706.
Grabmann, M.,
   "Thomas von Aquin — eine Einführung in seine Persönlichkeit und
   Gedankenwelt," Munich (1920).
Gutwenger, E.,
   "Der Begriff der Natur in der Theologie," *ZeitKathTheol* 75 (1953),
   pp. 461-464.
Hein, N. J., Würthwein, E., et al
   "Gnade Gottes," *Die Religion in Geschichte und Gegenwart*, Tübin-
   gen (1958) 2, pp. 1630-1645.
Huby, J.,
   "Foi et contemplation d'après s. Thomas," *RechScRel* 9 (1919),
   pp. 136-162.
Kenny, J. P.,
   i) "Created actuation by the uncreated Act . . . ," *The Australasian
   Catholic Record* 27 (1950), pp. 130-141; 210-223.
   ii) "Beatific Vision" *AustCathRecord* 31 (1954), pp. 106-118; 212-
   222.
   iii) "Reflections on human nature and the Supernatural," *Theol-*

Studies 14 (1953), pp. 280-287.

iv) "Temple and temples of the Holy Ghost," *The Heythrop Journal* 2 (1961), pp. 318-332.

v) "Grace here — glory there," *The Clergy Monthly* 27 (1963), pp. 54-59.

Kösters, R.,

"Die Lehre von der Rechtfertigung . . . .," *ZeitKathTheol* 90 (1968), pp. 309-324.

Küng, H.,

Justification, London (1964).

Landgraf, M. M.,

Dogmengeschichte der Frühscholastik, Regensburg (1952-1956).

Leeming, B.,

"A master theologian: Fr. M. de la Taille," *The Month* (1934), pp. 31-41.

Lennerz, H.,

De Deo uno, Rome (1948), pp. 96-149.

Lonergan, B.,

"St. Thomas' thought on *gratia operans*," *Theological Studies* 2 (19-41), pp. 289-324, 3 (1942), pp. 69-88, 375-402, 533-578.

de Lubac, H.,

i) "Remarques sur l'histoire du mot surnaturel" *NouvRevTheol* 61 1934), pp. 225-249; 350-370.

ii) *Surnaturel,* Paris (1946).

iii) *Augustinianism and modern Theology,* London (1969).

iv) *The Mystery of the Supernatural,* London (1967).

v) *Athéisme et sens de l'homme,* (1968).

Malevez, L.,

"La gratuité du surnaturel," *NouvRevTheol* 75 (1953), pp. 561-586, 673-689.

Meehan, F. X.,

Efficient causality in Aristotle and St. Thomas, Washington (1940).

Meissner, W.,

Foundations for a Psychology of Grace, New Jersey (1966).

Mersch, E.,

Le corps mystique du Christ, Brussels (1936).

Michel, A.,

"Surnaturel," DTC 14, 2849-2859.

Moeller, C., Philips, G.,
The Theology of Grace and the Ecumenical Movement, London (1961).
Morency, R.,
L'union de grâce selon s. Thomas, Montreal (1950).
Meyer, C.,
A Contemporary Theology of Grace, New York (1971).
Oberman, H.,
The Harvest of Medieval Theology, Massachusetts (1963).
O'Connor, W.,
i) "A new concept of Grace and the supernatural," *The Ecclesiastical Review*, 98 (1938), pp. 401-414.
ii) "The theory of the supernatural," *TheolStudies* 3 (1942), pp. 403-412.
Oddone, A.,
I Problemi della grazia divina, Milan (1937).
Oman, J.,
Grace and Personality, London (1962).
Petavius, D.,
Dogmata Theologica, Vivès, Paris (1865) 3.
Philipp, W.,
"Natur und Übernatur," *Rel in Gesch und Gegenwart*, Tübingen (1960) 4, pp. 1329-1332.
Phillipe, M. D.,
Mystère du corps mystique du Christ, Paris (1959).
Pope, H.,
"The beatific vision of God," *God*, ed. C. Lattey, London (1931).
Rahner, K.,
i) *Theological Investigations*, London (1961), 1 esp. 4th, 9th & 10th essays.
ii) *Theological Investigations*, London (1963), 2 esp. 1st, 3rd, 4th, 5th & 6th essays.
iii) *Theological Investigations*, London (1966) 4 "On the theology of the incarnation" 105-120; "Questions of controversial theology on Justification" 189-218.
iv) *Nature and Grace*, London (1963).
de Régnon, Th.,
La métaphysique des causes d'après s. Thomas et Albert le Grand, Paris (1906).

Renwart, L.,
"La *natura pura* à la lumière de l'encyclique, *Humani generis,*"
NouvRevTheol 74 (1952), pp. 337-354.
Retailleau, M.,
La sainte Trinité dans les Ames justes, Angers (1932).
Rivière, J.,
"Justification," DTC 8, 2077-2227.
Rondet, H.,
i) *The Grace of Christ,* New York (1966).
ii) *Essais sur la théológie de la grâce,* Paris (1964).
Rousselot, P.,
i) "Les yeux de la foi," *RechScRel* 1 (1910), pp. 241-260.
ii) "... la notion de foi naturelle," *RechScRel* 3 (1913), pp. 1-37.
Schillebeeckx, E.,
Concept of Truth and Theological Renewal, London (1968).
Schoonenberg, P.,
Covenant and Creation, London (1968).
Seckler, M.,
Instinkt und Glaubensville nach Thomas von Aquin, Mainz (1961).
de la Taille, M.,
i) "The Schoolmen," *The Incarnation,* Cambridge (1926), pp. 152-190.
ii) "Actuation créé par acte incréé ...," *RechScRel* 18 (1928), pp. 253-269.
iii) "Entretien amical ... sur la grâce d'union," *Revue Apologetique* 58 (1929), pp. 5-27, 129-146.
Teilhard de Chardin, P.,
i) *Le Milieu Divin,* London (1966).
ii) *The Phenomenon of Man,* London (1969).
iii) *The Future of Man,* London (1969).
Terrien, J. B.,
La grâce et la gloire, Paris (1901).
Trüstsch
Ss. Trinitatis inhabitatio apud theologos recentiores, Rome (1946).
Vollert, C.,
Review of de Lubac's *Surnaturel, TheolStudies* 8 (1947), pp. 288-294.